Investor State Arbitration in a Changing World Order

International Investment Law and Arbitration

Volumes published in this Brill Research Perspectives title are listed at *brill.com/rpi*

Investor State Arbitration in a Changing World Order

By

Alexander W. Resar and Tai-Heng Cheng

BRILL

LEIDEN | BOSTON

This paperback book edition is simultaneously published as issue 3.2–3 of *International Investment Law a*
Arbitration, DOI:10.1163/24055778-12340009.

Library Congress Control Number: 2021936792

Typeface for the Latin, Greek, and Cyrillic scripts: "Brill". See and download: brill.com/brill-typeface.

ISBN 978-90-04-39058-4 (paperback)
ISBN 978-90-04-39059-1 (e-book)

This book is printed on acid-free paper and produced in a sustainable manner.

Contents

Investor State Arbitration in a Changing World Order

Alexander W. Resar
Quinn Emanuel Urquhart & Sullivan, LLP
alexresar@gmail.com

Tai-Heng Cheng
International Arbitration and Trade
Sidley Austin LLP
tcheng@sidley.com

Abstract

In *Investor State Arbitration in a Changing World Order*, the authors examine the sustained worldwide challenges to investor state arbitration arising from across the political spectrum. These challenges have led to extensive and thoughtful proposals for reform from the international arbitration community, domestic lawmakers, and international bureaucrats. These reforms play an important role in the continuous evolution of investor state arbitration, and will enhance the quality of justice rendered. However, the authors argue, these reforms are insufficient to resolve the domestic political challenges that investor state arbitration faces. Only political solutions that justify for broad populations the international flow of capital and the independent resolution of disputes arising therefrom can preserve the institution of investor state arbitration. Absent the more equitable distribution of the benefits associated with the international flow of capital, political support for investor state arbitration will remain tenuous, notwithstanding the significant de-escalatory benefits investor state arbitration offers.

Keywords

legitimacy – international law – investment arbitration – trade law

 | DOI:10.1163/9789004390591_002

Preface

We are both legatees of Yale Law School's New Haven approach to international law, having studied with Professor W. Michael Reisman two decades apart. We thought it would be a fruitful exercise to collaborate, applying the common intellectual tools we were gifted to a contemporary global issue.

We did not aim to write a tome. Rather, we sought to address succinctly an international legal issue that persists beyond whatever fashionable problem might capture the imagination of policy makers and the legal profession from season to season. The problem we chose to examine is the sustained worldwide attack on investor state arbitration. Investor state arbitration is a global system to resolve disputes between foreign investors and the host states in which the investors transfer large amounts of capital over extended time periods. Given the importance of this system to world order, our project seemed like a worthwhile endeavor to undertake.

The criticisms of investor state arbitration have garnered widespread attention. They have also led to extensive and thoughtful responses from the international arbitration community, domestic lawmakers, and international bureaucrats. There is a place for all the proposals for reform. We expect that many of these proposals, properly implemented, will improve the system of investor state arbitration.

However, in our view, in order for investor state arbitration to thrive as an effective global system of dispute resolution and not merely to continue to survive as a little used relic of the past, the deeper normative concerns of the political movements against investor state arbitration must be addressed. Domestic constituents will continue to exert pressure on elected officials to reject investor state arbitration, unless the foreign investment that this system is designed to promote leads to wealth and well-being for broad populations, and not only business elites. In every country, this is a national project rather than an international one. However, the failure of domestic political bodies to equitably distribute wealth does not justify the rejection of an institution that helps to make resources available for development, and promotes peaceful and de-politicized resolution of international economic disputes. Accordingly, on the global scale, we continue to believe that investor-state arbitration should be widely adopted.

Although we started working on the manuscript in 2017, by the time we completed this manuscript in January 2020, the world was in the throes of the Covid-19 pandemic. The attention of elected officials, lawyers and arbitrators has rightly focused on how to get through this world crisis. But while the criticisms against investor-state arbitration have subsided as the world's attention is focused elsewhere, those criticisms have not gone away. They remain, and will return, until they are addressed.

The pandemic has reminded us all that nations cannot solve global problems alone. This lesson applies equally to the movement of capital across nations. There must be an effective international solution to de-escalate conflicts regarding international capital and the returns that are promised in exchange for this captal. It is imperative to maintain and restore order in international trade and investment when conflicts arise. Populist movements today may not remember the horrors of gunboat diplomacy from prior centuries, or the failure of the Calvo Doctrine in Latin America, which attempted to force foreign investors to obtain relief from the national governmental bodies that may have violated the foreign investors' rights in the first place. These alternatives, which are what the world community will be left with without investor-state arbitration in some form, are even more sub-optimal.

Like democracy, investor state arbitration may be the least bad system. For this reason, it is our hope that this monograph encourages all stakeholders to focus not only on addressing the mechanical defects of investor-state arbitration, but also to consider the domestic socio-economic reforms necessary to provide the political will necessary to keep alive, and thriving, investor state arbitration as a global system of dispute resolution.

January 3, 2020

Tai-Heng Cheng
Tuxedo Park, New York

Alexander W. Resar
New York, New York

Introduction: The Intertwined Fates of the Liberal Order and Investor-State Arbitration

Since its inauguration in the Washington Convention in 1965, the institution of investor state arbitration ("ISA") has enhanced the availability of capital for the development of resources in states across the world, while replacing politically-fraught interstate conflicts with a peaceful mechanism for the resolution of disputes arising from those capital investments. The increased flow of capital across national boundaries has occurred under the broader proliferation of bilateral and multilateral investment and trade agreements, reflecting the expanding volume and of global trade.[1]

Many of these free trade and investment agreements contain ISA provisions, enabling foreign investors to initiate disputes against host states for violating their obligations to foreign investors before neutral and independent arbitrators. At the most basic level, ISA enables foreign investors to seek compensation for a state's violations of investor protections as defined by treaty without requiring recourse in the judiciaries of the host states, which may by more likely to favor their own national governments or have even played a role in the challenged state conduct. Instead, ISA provides for the resolution of such legal disputes before arbitrators, whether selected on an ad hoc basis or obtained from a permanent roster of a supranational quasi-judicial body, wholly independent from any nation's judiciary.

The existence of ISA as the preferred mechanism for enforcing a states' obligations to foreign investors depends upon states' willful accession to investment agreements containing ISA provisions, and thus upon political support for the institution. Unlike commercial arbitration, which emerges out of contract and thus requires only agreement between the contracting parties, ISA emerges out of international treaties and thus requires support or approval from the political bodies of the states party to the treaties.

Recently, political support for ISA has cratered. While traditionally capital-importing states only ever granted the institution the tepid acceptance necessary for reaching agreements with their capital-exporting trade partners, even the traditionally capital-exporting states, which provided ISA the affirmative support necessary for its widespread adoption by insisting on the inclusion of ISA provisions in investment agreements, have shown increasing skepticism towards ISA. This hesitance on the part of capital-exporting states is apparent where, at least, those capital-exporting states have ceased including ISA

1 See U.N. Conference on Trade and Development ("UNCTAD"), Bilateral Investment Treaties in the Mid-1990s, at 18–19, U.N. Doc. UNCTAD/ITE/IIT/7, U.N. Sales No. E.98.II.D.8 (1998) [hereinafter UNCTAD Report] (describing exponential increase in bilateral investment treaties); *see also* Jan Paulsson, *International Arbitration and the Generation of Legal Norms*, Transnat'l Di. Mgmt., (2006), at 5 n.3 (noting "prodigious expansion of international commercial arbitration in the past half-century"); Catherine Rogers, *Emerging Dilemmas in International Economic Arbitration: The Vocation of the International Arbitrator*, 20 AM. U. INT'L L. REV. 957, 965 (2005) ("With the explosion in international trade and, consequently, trade-related disputes, the field of international arbitrators experienced significant expansion and diversification in the past two decades."); Luke Eric Peterson, Bilateral Investment Treaties and Development Policy-Making 1–2, available at http://www.iisd.org/pdf/2004/trade-bits.pdf (describing increase in bilateral investment treaties ("BITS") across the world).

provisions in investment agreements and, at most, expressly refused to accede to investment agreements containing ISA provisions. And this reluctance is not merely a function of rising economic nationalist sentiment; although ISA has fallen victim to the broader blowback against trade agreements and the global free flow of capital, the institution itself faces significant criticism. That criticism predates the rise of economic nationalism in the 2010s. In democratic capital-exporting states, this reluctance to embrace ISA, particularly in agreements involving multiple traditionally capital-exporting states, reflects a lack of political support for the institution of ISA. In short, the institution of ISA must generate additional political support to survive, or it will become a relic of past trade and investment agreements, to be invoked less and less frequently by investors until those agreements have been replaced.

The challenges to generating political support for ISA are significant; the institution faces criticism from the emerging nationalist right, which opposes the exportation of capital writ large, and the political left and center, which challenge the institution's democratic legitimacy. Adopting a mercantilist, zero-sum view of international trade in which exported capital deprives the investor's home state of the developmental benefits that could accrue from investment, the nationalist right purports to question the very promotion of foreign investment that ISA assumes as its justification: why enhance protections for investment made abroad instead of promoting domestic investment? The democracy-deficit criticism of ISA, on the other hand, questions the legitimacy of delegating judicial power to private actors: why grant private actors de facto absolute power over a state's regulatory decisions?

Because these challenges to ISA refute the fundamental state-endorsed components of ISA, specifically the promotion of foreign investment and private resolution of disputes arising from those investments, these criticisms threaten both the legitimacy and long-term viability of ISA to an extent unacknowledged by the institution of ISA, which has largely concerned itself with minor modifications and refinements to the practice and standards of ISA. Indeed, proposals to reform ISA, both through incremental tweaks and systemic changes, abound. But these proposals will do little to ensure the durability of ISA absent political support that requires acceptance and approval of the fundamental goals and means of ISA. Lawyers, academics, trade-negotiators, and the other architects of the institution of ISA have so far been reluctant to engage these challenges to the legitimacy of the institution itself.

To an extent underappreciated by even the architects of the institution of ISA, then, the survival of that institution is beyond its own control, depending upon the survival of the architecture of the liberal international order to which ISA is affixed. Though ISA understands itself as a self-correcting system, capable of frequent adaptations necessary to resolve singular problematic outcomes, these corrections resolve only internal inconsistencies. Even the systemic reforms intended to create a permanent investment court and appellate body proposed by, amongst others, the European Commission, fail to mollify either political challenge to the institution of ISA. The systemic reforms still assume the protection of foreign investment is a worthy goal, thus ignoring the challenge posed by the nationalist right. The reforms similarly neglect the left's challenge to ISA, as merely embedding the judicial form within supranational bodies that themselves face significant democratic legitimacy challenges, will do little to imbue ISA with the hard-won democratic legitimacy the institution of judicial review attained over centuries or shroud ISA in the democratic legitimacy supranational political institutions, including the European Union, still struggle for today.

Whether systemic or incremental, the existing reforms to the institution of ISA are only justifiable from a perspective internal to ISA. The proposed modifications may indeed enhance the reasoning and consistency of ISA's output (arbitral awards), but neither the quality nor consistency of arbitral awards are the target of the fundamentally political challenges to ISA. Although worth pursuing as part of a process to enhance the quality of justice afforded to states and investors, such reforms will not save ISA from its challengers, which, following *Achmea*, include even the supranational bodies that certain models of ISA seek to emulate.

Though the nationalist right's criticism of trade lacks consistency in application, and coherency in formulation, both of these challenges to the institution of ISA pose significant threats to the institution's existence. As demonstrated by the United States' formal withdrawal from the Trans-Pacific Partnership, which would have expanded and harmonized commitments and protections afforded to investors across a significant segment of the global economy, the nationalist right's objection poses a significant threat to the durability and continued progression of ISA. Similarly, the left's challenge to the democratic legitimacy of ISA has generated significant sympathy or express endorsement from leaders in the Democratic Party in the United States, labor parties across Europe, and socialist parties across the capital-importing world. Because the targets of both criticisms of ISA are intrinsic to the institution (the promotion of foreign investment, and the independent resolution of disputes arising therefrom), ISA will not be able to attain durable legitimacy solely through incremental or even systemic reforms that retain the fundamental characteristics of ISA.

The legitimization and long-term survival of ISA then turns on the capacity of the governments promoting the institution of ISA to address these challenges, and justify politically the commitments to foreign investors that those investors then enforce through ISA. Historically, the institution of ISA freed capital-importing states from the threat of economic (or even military) coercion for the protection of investment, while facilitating the presumably neutral and, diplomatically inexpensive protection of a capital-exporting state's foreign investments. ISA thus enhanced the quantity and quality of foreign direct investment necessary for the development of capital-importing states, as investors would more freely invest absent the risk associated with an investment that could only be recovered through coercive measures should the political tides shift against foreign investment in the host state.

The historical justifications for those commitments remain apt, and the democratic acceptance of those commitments remain attainable through the usual channels: only when the gains of enhanced investment facilitated by ISA are more equitably distributed across society will the institution of ISA provide its architects with the instrumental justifications necessary for the institution's durability. This necessary redistribution presents a national, rather than international, legal task, and accordingly cannot be resolved by even drastic or systemic reform of the institution of ISA, as we will attempt to show.

In Part 1, we detail the emergency of the institution of ISA, the political and legal context out of which ISA emerged, and the compact between capital-exporting and capital-importing states that ISA sought to embody.[2] The disproportionate accumulation of capital and distribution of resources between states facilitated the development of foreign direct investment as a means of supplying capital for the development of resources in under-capitalized states. While customary international law provided certain minimum standards for the protection of foreigners and their property, including their investments, in all but a few instances those foreign nationals were left without a means to enforce those minimum standards against the capital-importing states. Foreign investors could seek relief in the judiciaries of the host states, but those judiciaries could be susceptible to pressure from the host state government or even involved in the challenged conduct.

So after or instead of seeking relief in the courts of the host states, foreign investors relied upon their own states to protect their investments in presumable accordance with the customary international law of the time. This system of "diplomatic protection" was highly imprecise, and provided both too much and too little protection. From the perspective of the foreign investors, the system was frequently inadequate or at least highly unpredictable. Because foreign

---

2 *See* W. Michael Reisman, *The Past and Future of the Great Compact*, 33 ICSID Rev. 1, 56 (2018).

investors relied upon diplomatic (or even military) action by their own states for protection of their investments, only the politically-connected investors obtained protection, creating additional risk and increasing the cost of capital supplied by less-connected foreign investors. And from the perspective of the capital-importing states, the system of diplomatic protection merely subjected them to the whims of foreign states. Indeed, the system of diplomatic protection encouraged abuse by politically-connected investors in capital-exporting states, as those states determined unilaterally whether an investment was worthy of protection regardless of the true strength of the investors' claim, and the oft-disproportionate protections the capital-exporting state would provide.

When the system of diplomatic protection was challenged by predominantly Latin American, capital-importing states, the Second Peace Conference at The Hague embraced the beginning of an arbitration system; in exchange for limitations on the use of force by capital-exporting states to protect investments or collect debts, capital-importing states would agree to submit to arbitration between the debtor-state and creditor at the request of the creditor's state.[3] While capital-importing states, often newly-recognized in light of the decline of the European empires following the First and Second World Wars, initially rejected foreign investment with its generally Western origins and neo-colonial overtones, these states came to recognize "direct foreign investment as an indispensable means for assisting in national development."[4] The 1965 Washington Convention emerged out of this recognition, institutionalizing ISA through the World Bank's International Centre for Settlement of Investment Disputes (ICSID). The Washington Convention introduced the final structural development to resolving these disputes in form of the institution of ISA, which fully excised the capital-exporting state's role in the arbitration through the introduction of investor-initiated arbitrations resolved before arbitral tribunals. This history illustrates the purposes of ISA, and the international order to which ISA was affixed.

An assessment of ISA's purposes and broader theoretical commitments is necessary to understand the emerging challenges to the institution of ISA, addressed in Part 2, where we will catalogue the most threatening challenges to the institution of ISA, delineating by political origin and target. We argue that the two most prominent, and thus threatening, challenges to ISA emerge from two distinct political contexts, and thus take as their target two distinct but fundamental components of ISA. Where the paradoxically global nationalist right challenges the aim of ISA (enhanced foreign direct investment),

---

3 *Id.*

4 *Id.* at 59.

the democratic legitimacy challenge from the left contests the legitimacy of the mechanism promoting foreign direct investment: arbitration before private actors apart from the state. We first address the nationalist right's challenge to foreign investment, international trade, and even liberalism writ large, as both capital-importing and capital-exporting states have retrenched in their commitment to ISA as the preferred mechanism for the protection of foreign direct investment. In capital-importing states, the national right expresses reluctance to exchange their resources for foreign capital, intimating a return to the pre-Washington Convention but post World War II era in which newly-independent states sought to develop their own resources independent from the influence of foreign capital.

More surprising is the neo-mercantilist right in capital-exporting states, such as the United States under administration of President Trump, who understood the exportation of capital as a zero-sum competition, one in which the United States should discourage the exportation of capital as lost opportunity for the investor's home state. The neo-mercantilist nationalist right in the United States, for example, does not oppose foreign investment in the United States, and even actively pursues foreign direct investment as a source of jobs and prosperity, but understands itself as in competition with other states for foreign direct investments and its benefits. Even while it actively courts foreign direct investment, then, the nationalist right in the United States opposes government efforts to promote the exportation of its own capital, including the institution of ISA that is criticized as providing political risk-insurance for investors to pursue outsized returns outside the country. The inconsistency in application and incoherency in formulation undermine the nationalist right's challenge to the institution of ISA, but the challenge nonetheless exposes potential weaknesses in the public's support for the promotion of foreign investment in both capital-exporting states, where the nationalist right opposes the exportation of capital even while actively courting the importation of capital, and capital-importing states, where the nationalist right opposes foreign investment as efforts by outsiders to control the states' resources.[5] This explication

5 A similar theoretical inconsistency underpinned many of the arguments raised by the nationalist right during the campaign for the United Kingdom to leave the European Union. The nationalist right targeted as undemocratic and illegitimate the regulations that facilitated the flow of trade between the United Kingdom, while promising that to retain the economic benefits of such trade through the creation of more favorable bilateral trade and investment agreements. In both the United States and United Kingdom, then, despite being framed theoretically as a challenge to the very possibility of exporting capital and resources, the nationalist rights' challenge to foreign trade and investment took aim in practice more at each State's specific trade and investment allocations.

of the challenge that the nationalist right poses to ISA forms much of Section One in Part 2.

In Section Two of Part 2, we address the challenge to the democratic legitimacy of ISA's delegation of what amounts to judicial power to private actors. The left challenges the legitimacy of private actors issuing decisions that are binding and difficult-to-reverse on state actors. The institution of ISA is at its most illegitimate, according to this challenge, when private arbitrators grant protections to foreign investors based upon determinations that a state violated its own (presumably unsettled) law because these decisions usurp a state's ability to determine through democratic means the content and form of its own laws. The institution of ISA lacks democratic legitimacy even when presiding over disputes exclusively concerning a state's violation of its international obligations because ISA delegates to private actors effective control over a state's regulatory decisions, or so this challenge claims. While this challenge to the institution of ISA could have arisen at the institution's founding in the 1965 Washington Convention, it was only after the traditionally capital-exporting states also became subject to investor-initiated arbitrations that the left in traditionally capital-exporting states began to call into question the purported democratic illegitimacy of the institution. Only when the sovereignty of traditionally capital-importing states came under threat did this opposition to the institution of ISA gain political force, as the states that had affirmatively advanced the institution of ISA by fighting for its inclusion in trade and investment agreements grew disenchanted with the system they had wrought.[6]

Indeed, even supranational bodies like the European Union, themselves subject to similar legitimization challenges, have adopted elements of the democratic-legitimacy critique of ISA when reining in its excesses. In *Achmea*, for example, the European Court of Justice held that arbitral tribunals were inappropriate bodies to conclusively resolve questions of European Union law, because at least when constituted on an ad hoc basis, such tribunals are insufficiently grounded within the national judiciaries approved by the European Court of Justice.[7]

---

6 *See* Alvarez, Guillermo Aguilar & Park, William W., *The New Face of Investment Arbitration: NAFTA Chapter 11*, 28 Yale J. Int'l L. 365, 366 (2003) (explaining that while, "[l]ike many other industrialized nations, the United States has traditionally favored arbitration for resolution of investment disputes with foreign host states, particularly with respect to expropriation claims," a significant backlash against ISA has emerged as the United States became a frequent respondent in investor-initiated arbitrations).

7 *See, generally*, Andre Janssen and Christian Johannes Wahnschaffe, *For Whom the Bell Tolls: Any Hope Left for Investment Arbitration After* Achmea?, Dispute Resolution in China, Europe and World (ed. Lei Chen and Andre Janssen) (Springer 2020).

In Part 3, we address certain key proposed reforms, both systemic and incremental, to the institution of ISA circulating amongst States in proposed model investment agreements, and intergovernmental organizations and academics in yet-to-be adopted proposals for future investment agreements. Specifically, we address efforts that states have made towards the creation of independent and permanent trial and appellate bodies, efforts to enhance the transparency of ISA proceedings, and efforts to refine or reformulate the obligations that states owe investors under their investment agreements. In surveying these proposed reforms, we address the reforms' capacity to resolve the challenges to the institution of ISA posed by both the nationalist right and the left. And we conclude that these proposals are inadequate to resolve the existential threat ISA faces. Although existing reform proposals may improve the quality or consistency of arbitral awards (a worthwhile goal from the internal perspective that assumes both the worthiness of arbitration as a means to promote foreign investment) these reforms fail to imbue with legitimacy either the practice of delegating to private actors authority over a state's regulatory decisions or the promotion of foreign investment. If the proposed reforms are indeed intended to preserve the institution of ISA, and the political challenges addressed above threaten the institution of ISA, then the proposed reforms fail.

We conclude by arguing that the preservation of the institution of ISA depends upon the ability of both traditionally capital-importing and capital-exporting states' to complete political tasks of a national rather than international nature. Across the liberal world, the institution of ISA requires democratic support. Politically-connected businesses, including the largest resource extraction and infrastructure development companies, support ISA and will continue to do so for as long as foreign investment remains profitable. But widespread democratic support requires that the benefits of increased foreign investment be shared more equitably across society.

This may prove an impossible task, rendering perilous ISA's prospects for survival. There exist significant theoretical[8] and empirical[9] challenges to the unrestrained flow of capital. Even assuming foreign direct investment promotes meaningful economic development, the role of investment agreements

8 *See* Jagdish Bhagwati, *The Capital Myth: The Difference Between Trade in Widgets and Dollars*, FOREIGN AFF., May–June 1998, at 7 (arguing the theoretical defense of free trade across national boundaries does not similarly justify the free flow of capital across national boundaries).

9 *See* THOMAS PIKETTY, LE CAPITAL AU XXI SIECLE 120–21 (2013) (disputing hypothesis that foreign direct investment and free flow of capital played a significant role in the rapid growth and development of the East Asian economies).

in facilitating the flow those investments remains contested.[10] Should any of these challenges prove meritorious, the liberal investment order, premised upon the relatively unrestrained flow of capital will become untenable. So, too, will the institution of investor-state arbitration, which aims above all to decrease the risks and costs associated with foreign investment, and thus enhance its availability.

Even if the empirical and theoretical defenses of the international economic order premised upon the availability and free flow of capital prevail upon experts and technocrats, that victory may prove insufficient to sustain the institution of ISA in democratic states without broader political support. The expansive role taken on by arbitral tribunals presiding over investor-initiated suits, requiring application of international legal norms and, controversially, interpretation of the host state's own law or even the law of supranational bodies like the European Union, requires legitimation that exceeds the merely instrumental account of ISA as enhancing the flow of investment.[11] And that broader political support depends not upon the reasoning or transparency of any particular arbitral award, but the ability of governments to generate political support for the liberal economic order by more equitably distributing the gains and prosperity that order has wrought across their populations.[12] In short, the institution of ISA rests upon infirm ground; the ISA's capacity for self-correction and reform will not generate the support necessary for its survival (though such efforts to optimize the system should no doubt continue), as the institution's fate rests upon the liberal order of which ISA is part and parcel.

---

10 See Christian Bellak, *How Bilateral Investment Treaties Impact on Foreign Direct Investment: A Meta-Analysis of Public Policy* (2013), *available* at http://www2.gre.ac.uk/__data/assets/pdf_file/0006/822705/Christian-Bellak-How-BilateralInvestment-Treaties-Impact-on-Foreign-Direct-Investment-A-Meta-analysis-of-Public-Policy.pdf ("In a nutshell, the positive impact of BITs on FDI has not been confirmed empirically").

11 Kingsbury, Benedict, and Schill, Stephan, *Investor-State Arbitration as Governance: Fair and Equitable Treatment, Proportionality and the Emerging Global Administrative Law*, TDM 2 (2011) at 50 ("The common proposition that it is justified because it vindicates State aspirations to promote investment flows, if it does indeed do that, addresses only the ordinary functional conception of the tribunals as enforcing commitments and resolving disputes. It is a tenuous justification at best for the more far-reaching governance functions exercised by tribunals.").

12 *See* Eric A. Posner, *Liberal Internationalism and the Populist Backlash*, 49 Ariz. St. L. J. 795, 813 (2018) ("What went wrong? The simple answer is that the benefits of globalization—greater wealth and freedom—failed to materialize as promised, with most of the gains going to a small fragment of the global elite, or to vast populations of workers in places like China, with cheaper consumer goods in the West failing to compensate people in their minds for the economic dislocation they experienced.").

Part 1: The Development of Investor-State Arbitration

Before addressing the challenges to the institution of ISA, we first trace the development of ISA as the now-preferred mechanism for the protection of foreign investments. This history of the institution of ISA will illustrate the purposes of ISA and the structures of the international economic order to which ISA was affixed. The three sections in this Part therefore trace ISA's development. We follow ISA from the institution's state-to-state arbitration precursors in an era characterized predominantly by diplomatic protection through to the present era, where the traditionally capital-importing states behind the expansion of ISA have become subject to investor-initiated disputes and turned, at least rhetorically, against ISA.

The institution of ISA developed as a peaceful mechanism to enforce the protections under international law, whether customary or treaty-based, that a state must afford the property of foreign nationals.[13] ISA purported to provide a fair and neutral dispute mechanism that could lower the political and economic costs of protections for a foreign investor enforced at the state-to-state level. Before ISA's development, foreign nationals were left with only two choices to enforce a capital-importing state's obligations with regards to the protection of foreign investors. First, foreign investors could seek to enforce a host state's obligations through the judicial or political avenues available in that state. The host state's judicial and political avenues for relief presented an unpalatable option for investors when the obligations they are seeking to enforce have purportedly been violated by the very judicial or political actors who would then preside over the dispute. Second, foreign investors could turn to the government of their own states to provide protection for their investments through the many avenues of state-to-state diplomacy. Protection afforded to investments of a state's nationals abroad occurred pursuant to the customary international law of the time through a system termed "diplomatic protection," as state-to-state diplomatic procedures, including even the threat of military force, protected the politically-connected foreign national's investment.[14] Investors frequently opted for the latter form of protection to the extent their political connections permitted, and in this system of diplomatic protection, the capital exporting states exerted economic or even military coercion over capital-importing states to ensure the protection of the property and investments of the politically-connected investors capable of mobilizing their national governments.

13 *See* Reisman, *supra* note 2 at 56.

14 *Id.*

When capital-importing states began to challenge this system, and the increased costs of military and economic coercion rendered capital-exporting states less inclined to continue to pursue coercive protections for their nationals' foreign investments, arbitration emerged as a potential solution. Instead of enforcing the capital-exporting state's preferences on the capital-importing state through coercive means of international statecraft, the two states would resolve their dispute before independent adjudicatory bodies. Initially, arbitration served to mediate the claims of the investor's home state and the capital-importing state. This form of state-to-state arbitration, however, retained the international political dimensions present in any state-to-state dispute. Only following the innovation of investor-initiated arbitration before independent adjudicatory bodies did the modern institution of ISA emerge. ISA thus embodied a compact in which capital-exporting states excised the threat of diplomatic coercion in exchange for their nationals to obtain the rights to initiate investment disputes against capital-importing states to be adjudicated by independent and impartial arbitrators.[15]

Though the rise of ISA is a recent phenomenon in international economic history, we can already divide the institution's existence into two distinct periods defined by the characterization of the states responding to investor initiated claims. The compact reached between capital-importing and capital-exporting states marks the first period, as investors from capital-exporting states initiated suits against capital-importing states to ensure the protection of their investments. Though some capital-importing states expressed reluctance to participate in this arrangement, they understood acquiescence as the price that must be paid for access to the foreign capital that those states believed to be imperative for economic development. In this period, ISA worked as intended for both sides: host states seeking capital decreased the cost of that capital without subjecting the regulatory decisions of that states to the enforcement whims of a capital-exporting state, and the capital-exporting state no longer needed to initiate costly diplomatic proceedings to ensure the protection of its investors abroad.

But states did not confine ISA to the agreements between capital-importing and capital-exporting states for which the institution had been designed. Instead, the proliferation of multilateral investment and free trade agreements and inclusion of ISA provisions therein resulted in the availability of ISA to resolve disputes between foreign investors and traditionally capital-exporting states.[16] Accordingly, the spread of ISA to investment agreements between

15 *Id.*

16 *See, e.g.*, Rafael Leal-Arcas, *Proliferation of Regional Trade Agreements: Complementing or Supplanting Multilateralism*, 11 Chi. J. Int'l L. 597 (2011).

traditionally capital-exporting states in the form of multilateral trade agreements such as NAFTA marks the second period of the institution's existence.[17] Because nationals from these capital-exporting states invested in each other, and at times sought protection for their investments from the independent arbitrators that previously presided over disputes against developing and capital-importing states, an entirely new class of respondent states emerged.

Subjecting traditionally capital-exporting states to investor's claims presented a new threat to ISA's prospects for survival, as investors neglected judicial systems presumed adequate by traditionally capital-exporting states to advance claims before independent arbitrators. Instead of granting private actors quasi-judicial powers over a capital-importing state's regulatory decisions, these investment agreements between or inclusive of traditionally capital-exporting states were now subjecting those states regulatory or judicial decisions to review by private actors. Unsurprisingly, challenges to the legitimacy of such a delegation of judicial or quasi-judicial power became significantly more threatening to the institution of ISA. The challenge to ISA now emerged from the capital-exporting states who previously guaranteed ISA's existence by imposing such provisions in investment agreements from positions of negotiating strength upon capital-importing states desperate for the foreign direct investment believed to be necessary for development.

Simultaneously, a neo-mercantilist populist and nationalist right has emerged in both traditionally capital-importing and capital-exporting states, challenging the desirability of foreign control of resources in the former states and the outward flow of funds that could otherwise produce wealth domestically in the latter states. The sections that follow will place both of these political challenges to the institution of ISA in context by tracing ISA's emergence and development over the past three centuries.

1 *Diplomatic Protection and Early Investment Arbitration*

The earliest mechanism for the protection of the foreign investments made by the nationals of a state emerged in the seventieth century, where states could elect to protect those investments through the available tools of international statecraft, including diplomacy, negotiation, and economic or military coercion.[18] This state-dependent mechanism for the protection of foreign investment became known as "diplomatic protection", or, in the rarer instances

---

17 *See* Alvarez & Park, *supra* note 6 at 365.

18 See Kate Miles, The Origins of International Investment Law: Empire, Environment and the Safeguarding of Capital (2013).

in which states rely upon military coercion, "gunboat diplomacy."[19] Diplomatic protection, however, provided inadequate protection from an investor's perspective, as an investor's home government could not be ordered to initiate diplomatic protections.[20] This inability to guarantee protections created significant risk, especially for investors lacking political connections. And even those investors confident in their capacity to call upon their home state's governments to protect their foreign investments would be required to expend the resources necessary to lobby the government for action. Accordingly, while preferred by investors in the absence of any alternative because "diplomatic protection" offered at least some form of protection, the cost of foreign capital remained high.

But diplomatic protection was also problematic from the capital-importing and capital-exporting states' perspective. From the capital-importing state's perspective, the threat of military coercion created a wildly disproportionate threat to sustain often exploitative economic arrangements founded upon the unequal economic engagements of the colonial era. The risk of military action in protection of foreign capital granted foreign investors a disproportionate level of control over government decisions of capital-importing states, resulting in extractive relationships that brought little benefit to host state's populace. And because the possibility for diplomatic retaliation flowed from the foreign investor's political influence rather than any established international norms, capital-importing states lacked any consistent legal backdrop against which they could regulate foreign investment with predictable response from the regulated parties.

And even from the capital-exporting state's perspective, the coercive measures necessary to recover a politically-connected national's investment potentially required the inefficient allocation of diplomatic resources. The protection of a national's foreign investments required the expenditure of diplomatic time and energy, and threatened to conflict with a state's foreign policy objectives. These potential inefficiencies only became more extreme as the costs of projecting military power increased over time, and provide one explanation for why states occasionally elected mediation or arbitration as a means to resolve disputes regarding the protections owed to their investors in a militarily comparable state.

---

19 See Grover Clark, *The English Practice with Regard to Reprisals by Private Persons*, 27 AM. J. INT'L L. 694, 695–96 (1933); Ray C. Jones, *NAFTA Chapter 11 Investor-to-State Dispute Resolution: A Shield to Be Embraced or a Sword to Be Feared?*, 2002 BYU L. Rev. 527, 529–31 (detailing transition from "gunboat diplomacy" to investor-state arbitration).

20 *Id.*

Though diplomatic protection reigned as the dominant mechanism by which capital-exporting states protected the investments of their nationals in more coercible states, arbitration existed in rare circumstances generally involving militarily-comparable states as a mechanism to protect a foreign national's investments without requiring foreign nationals to submit their claims to the judiciary of the state in which the investment was made.[21] Unlike modern ISA, however, these arbitrations occurred between states, and the foreign investor's state was required to initiate the arbitration on the investor's behalf.[22] The "Jay Treaty" of 1794,[23] for example, authorized the adjudication by five independent commissioners of claims brought by Great Britain on behalf of British creditors for property damage or losses suffered arising out of the American Revolution.[24] The Jay Treaty adopted a practice similar to modern ISA (albeit between two states rather than a foreign investor and a state), in which each state would nominate two commissioners and the fifth would be chosen unanimously by the other four commissioners. Similarly, in 1871, arbitration again played a significant role in resolving a dispute between the United States and Great Britain.[25] While this dispute concerned a violation of the laws of war rather than the protections to be afforded investors, the principle of a state-to-state dispute resolved before independent arbitrators developed at least in part from its predecessor under the Jay Treaty.[26]

While state-to-state arbitration placing both parties on equal terms emerged between comparable powers such as the United States and Great Britain toward the end of the 19th century, less neutral arbitral mechanisms for resolving state disputes were imposed upon Latin American states by capital-exporting European nations on behalf of their investors. Arbitrations conducted pursuant

---

21 *But see* Jason Webb Yackee, *The First Investor-State Arbitration: The Suez Canal Company v Egypt (1864)*, 17 J. WORLD INV. & TRADE 401 (2016).

22 Sergio Puig, *Recasting ICSID's Legitimacy Debate—Towards a Goal-Based Empirical Agenda*, 36 Ford. Int'l L. J. 465, 479–480 (2013) ("Thus, in theory, prior to the ICSID Convention, the cases involving property of aliens abroad were initially treated as domestic conflicts, unless the parties had agreed on compulsory arbitration. Only after spending economic, diplomatic, or military resources could international adjudication follow in a mercantilist (state-to-state) mode. Only states could bring claims following the formal rules derived from general international law, commonly known as exhaustion of local remedies, espousal of claims, and diplomatic protection.").

23 Treaty of Amity, Commerce and Navigation, Nov. 19, 1794, U.S.-Gr. Brit., 8 Stat. 116.

24 *See* Barton Legum, *Federalism, NAFTA Chapter Eleven and the Jay Treaty of 1794*, 95 AM. SOC. INT'L. L. PROC. 202 (2001).

25 Alabama Claims Case, Decision and Award (Sept. 14, 1872), reprinted in Thomas Willing Balch, The Alabama Arbitration, 131 app. (1900).

26 *Id.*

to these disputes reflected the coercive diplomacy of diplomatic protection far more than the current system of investor-state arbitrations, as European states forced Latin American states to submit their disputes to adjudication before other European sovereigns, who were strongly predisposed to rule in favor of their fellow colonial powers.[27] The arbitrations were conducted in Europe and by Europeans, resulting in investor-friendly outcomes.[28]

Given the limited availability of such arbitrations, biased adjudication when arbitration was available, and predominance of coercion, capital-importing states began to push back against the system of diplomatic protection.[29] Latin American countries, influenced by the jurisprudence of Carlos Calvo, began to challenge the availability of diplomatic protection, arguing that the principle of sovereignty precludes military or diplomatic interference by other states for the protection of their own investors, especially when those investors have elected to enter the capital-importing state and subject themselves to that state's laws.[30] The Calvo Doctrine, as it came to be called, acknowledged that foreign investors should not be treated differently than nationals, and thus should only seek protection in local courts so as not to avail themselves of rights and privileges inaccessible to nationals.[31]

At the turn of the century, another Argentinian, Luis M. Drago, published an influential letter challenging the British, German, and Italian naval blockade of Venezuelan ports in support of the collection of debts.[32] This blockade represented one of the more extreme instances in which the colonial powers exercised military force for the protection of foreign investments. Drago, then the Minister of Foreign Relations of Argentina, argued that public debt cannot justify military intervention by foreign powers. President Roosevelt of the United States, the recipient of Drago's letter as the self-appointed protector of the independence of the Americas from European coercion, reacted half-heartedly despite the United States' military dominance across the Americas. Roosevelt acknowledged the preference for a peaceful resolution to disputes arising from "the simply nonperformance of a contract with a private person." But, likely with the United States' own significant colonial business interests in mind, President Roosevelt simultaneously refused to disavow the use of force in response to "non-payment of public debts … [in] such circumstances of

27 *See* Alvarez & Park, *supra* note 6 at 367 (citing Lionel M. Summers, *Arbitration and Latin America*, 3 Cal. W. L. J. 1, 6–7 (2001)).
28 *Id.*
29 *See id.* at 368.
30 Jones, *supra* note 19 at 529–31.
31 *Id.*
32 *See* Reisman, *supra* note 2 at 56.

fraud and wrongdoing or violation of treaties ..."[33] Without the United States' support, the Pan-American Conference in 1906 failed to produce a treaty precluding the use of force for the protection of foreign investments or collection of debts, but did refer the matter to the Second Peace Conference at The Hague.[34]

This conference produced the Porter Convention,[35] which would lay the foundation for the compact between capital-importing and capital-exporting states that would eventually develop into the institution of investor-state arbitration.[36] While the Porter Convention reaffirmed the state-to-state nature of diplomatic protection, it granted capital-importing states the limitation on the use of force that Drago had advocated, requiring diplomatic rather than military solutions to disputes between capital-importing and capital-exporting states. Given the increasing costs of projecting military power and general decline of European colonialism both rendered the use of force for the preservation of investment interests less likely, this concession may have been more symbolic than a meaningful restraint. Regardless, in exchange for the recognition that foreign investors enjoyed unique protections, the capital-importing states acquiesced to mandatory arbitration before the Permanent Court of Arbitration.[37] The following section will explain how this initial commitment to an institutionalized mechanism for the protection of foreign nationals' investments developed into the institution of ISA.

33 *Id.* (citing Theodore Roosevelt, 'Sixth Annual Message to the Senate and House of Representatives' (3 December 1906) http://www.presidency.ucsb.edu/ws/?pid=29547).

34 *Id.*

35 *See, generally, id.* at 56; Hague Convention on the Limitation of Employment of Force for Recovery of Contract Debts (opened for signature 18 October 1907, entered into force 26 January 1910) ("Porter Convention").

36 *Id.*

37 *Id.* Citing the following language in the Porter Convention:

> The Contracting Powers agree not to have recourse to armed force for the recovery of contract debts claimed from the Government of one country by the Government of another country as being due to its nationals.
>
> This undertaking is, however, not applicable when the debtor State refuses or neglects to reply to an offer of arbitration, or, after accepting the offer, prevents any *compromise* from being agreed on, or, after the arbitration, fails to submit to the award.
>
> It is further agreed that the arbitration mentioned in paragraph 2 of the foregoing Article shall be subject to the procedure laid down in Part IV, Chapter 3, of The Hague Convention for the Pacific Settlement of International Disputes. The award shall determine, except where otherwise agreed between the parties, the validity of the claim, the amount of the debt, and the time and mode of payment.

2 *Institutionalized Investment Protections: Investor-State Arbitration*

Over the course of the 20th century, the state-to-state arbitration that the Porter Convention embraced as a replacement for diplomatic protection developed into the investor-initiated institution of ISA that exists today.[38] This transition did not occur seamlessly.

Following the collapse of the European empires, newly independent states sought a complete break from the colonial and extractive economic relationships of empire. In rejecting foreign political control, the newly-independent states simultaneously sought to minimize foreign economic control by subjecting any foreign investors to the absolute authority of the capital-importing state's judiciary.[39] To this effect, the 1974 U.N. Charter of Economic Rights and Duties of States stipulated that:

> each state has the right to nationalize, expropriate or transfer ownership of foreign property, in which case appropriate compensation should be paid by the state adopting such measures, taking into account its relevant laws and regulations and all circumstances that the state considers pertinent. In any case where the question of compensation gives rise to a controversy, it shall be settled under the domestic law of the nationalizing state and by its tribunals, unless it is freely and mutually agreed by all States concerned that other peaceful means be sought on the basis of the sovereign equality of States and in accordance with the principle of free choice of means.[40]

Newly-independent states re-embraced the Calvo Doctrine, requiring the submission of foreign nationals' investments disputes to the authority of the host states' judiciaries, and denying the premise of the Porter Convention: that foreign investors enjoyed unique protections otherwise unavailable to domestic suppliers of capital.

---

38 *Id.*

39 *See, e.g.*, UN General Assembly's Declaration on the Establishment of a New International Economic Order. GA Resolution A/RES/S-6/3201 (1 May 1974) and its Charter of Economic Right and Duties of States (CERDS), GA Resolution A/Res/40/182 (17 December 1984). *See also* Sergio Puig & Gregory Shaffer, *Imperfect Alternatives: Institutional Choice and the Reform of Investment Law*, 112 Am. J. Int'l L. 361, 364 (2018) (explaining that newly independent and developing states sought to create an economic order "that recognized their sovereign ownership of their natural resources and championed the exclusive use of domestic law and institutions").

40 G.A. Res. 3281, U.N. GAOR, 29th Sess., Supp. No. 31, at 50, U.N. Doc. A/9631 (1974).

The uncertainty regarding the protections a host state owed to foreign investors, if any, in light of these proclamations necessitated the investment agreements that clarified those obligations in the form of modern bilateral investment treaties ("BITS"). While the incentives for capital-exporting states to stem the tide of the Calvo Doctrine's reemergence are clear, it less immediately apparent why the newly-independent or otherwise developing nations would acquiesce to a return to the protections and obligations afforded to foreign investors in investment agreements. But the emerging economic nationalism in the newly independent states required economic progress; "the political imperative for elites in many of these states was to grow their national economies, increase the national wealth and, though some form of distribution, whether by provision of opportunity, entitlement or some mix of both, to expand the economic and other life opportunities of their citizens."[41] Whether democratic or authoritarian, then, economic development became a crucial basis for political legitimacy and necessitated, at least in the minds of developing states' governing bodies, the importation of foreign capital.[42]

Indeed, the economic-based model of political legitimacy dependent upon economic growth in turn required capital to fund promised developments. While the World Bank provided a significant source of public international funds for the reconstruction of Europe after the Second World War, the availability of international capital was insufficient to meet the demand and requirements of developing states.[43] That public international funds available through the World Bank were initially distributed primarily for the reconstruction of Europe after the Second World War also, no doubt, reflected the outsized influence of Europe and American on the post-war financial international financial institutions. Regardless, developing states required direct private foreign investment to make up for the shortfall. Recognizing this, both developed and developing states agreed to the 1965 Washington Convention, establishing the World Bank's International Centre for Settlement of Investment Disputes (ICSID), and introducing investor-initiated ISA as the preferred means for the protection of foreign investments. The compact embodied by the Washington Convention reflected the Porter Convention's excision of coercion in the form of diplomatic protection from the tools available to capital-exporting states in the protection of their nationals' investments.[44] Also as with the Porter Convention, capital-importing states acquiesced to the submission

41 Reisman, *supra* note 2 at 56.

42 *Id.*

43 *Id.*

44 *Id.*

of investment disputes to independent arbitration. Accordingly, at least for those states submitting to BITs containing ISA provisions, the renewed Calvo Doctrine of the 1974 U.N. Charter of Economic Rights and Duties of States was rendered hollow.

The crucial distinction between previous investor protections and the promise of the Washington Convention, however, concerned the process by which an investor initiated the dispute resolution mechanism. Previously, under the Porter Convention, an investor still relied upon the protection of her home state to enforce the obligations of a particular treaty or customary international law against the capital-exporting state through state-to-state arbitration. Under this model, an investor would still need to exercise political influence to encourage the investor's home state to support its claim and initiate (and then prosecute) the state-to-state arbitration on the investor's behalf. The Washington Convention, on the other hand, inaugurated an investor-initiated dispute resolution mechanism, ISA, in which the investor, rather than the investor's home state, could initiate the process by which an arbitral tribunal would be constituted to enforce a capital-importing state's obligations towards that investor.

The benefits of this investor-initiated solution are apparent for the foreign investor, as it no longer needed to rely upon political connections with the government of its home state to initiate the procedures for protection of its foreign investment, reducing uncertainty and increasing willingness to invest abroad.[45] The foreign investor would also be guaranteed a larger role in the

45 *See* Charles H. Brower II, *Structure, Legitimacy, and NAFTA's Investment Chapter*, 36 Vand. J. of Transnat'l L. 37, 89 (2003) (noting the general unavailability and unpredictability of state to state dispute settlement because states rarely initiate dispute resolution mechanisms, and "when they do, often base decisions on political expediency as opposed to the merits of claims."). For an explanation of the ways in which diplomatic protection disadvantages foreign investors, *see* Puig & Shaffer, *supra* note 39 at 388 ("Although diplomacy may work in some instances, it also can be complex, costly, and opaque. The more difficult that it is to understand channels of influence, the costlier it is for investors to organize for political action. Small- and medium-sized investors are likely to be particularly disadvantaged because they have less political access to state officials—who prioritize the deployment of state resources based on economic weight and systemic importance."). *But see* Jason Webb Yackee, *Pacta Sant Servanda and State Promises to Foreign Investors Before Bilateral Investment Treaties: Myth and Reality*, 32 FORDHAM INT'L L. J. 1550, 1610–11 (2008) ("My aim is simply to establish that developing countries enjoy significant flexibility to exit the BIT system – if they come to the conclusion that BITs are, on net, undesirable-without harming their ability to make binding commitments to investors on a case-by-case basis through investment contracts, supported by international arbitration."). Whether Brazil provides a meaningful refutation of the ability of investment agreements containing ISA provisions to increase the availability of foreign capital

arbitral process itself, able to prosecute its own case on its own behalf rather than relying on its home state at every stage of the arbitral process from the initiation of the proceeding to the appointment of arbitrators and presentation at hearing. For the capital-importing and capital-exporting states, the investor-initiated arrangement "depoliticized investment disputes," by transforming state-to-state disputes, with their attendant diplomatic costs, into investor-state disputes presumably governed exclusively by legal and economic considerations.[46]

But the creation of ISA in the Washington Convention did not guarantee the institution's immediate and widespread adoption.[47] The availability of ISA as a mechanism for the enforcement of obligations towards foreign investors depended upon the spread of BITs and multilateral investment agreements.[48] Initially, this spread was gradual and involved almost exclusively bilateral agreements between capital-exporting European states, and capital-importing, newly independent states seeking foreign capital.[49] In this way, the mechanism by which states implemented the protections afforded to foreign investors transitioned from the model of state-to-state arbitration embraced by the Porter Convention and prevalent in Treaties of Friendship, Commerce and Navigation to the investor-initiated ISA mechanism adopted by modern investment agreements.[50]

---

remains unclear; it is possible that Brazil has increased the cost of foreign capital by negotiating ad hoc arbitration agreements with particular foreign investors rather than with capital exporting states. Moreover, it is also possible that Brazil presents a sufficiently lucrative and large market for foreign investors to render logical investments even absent the protection of ISA provisions.

46 Puig, *supra* note 22 at 486 ("This individual-state mode of dispute settlement will reduce the possibility of abuse by powerful states by prohibiting the espousal of the claim, unless the respondent state fails to abide by and comply with the pecuniary obligations of the awards."). *See also* Reisman, *supra* note 2 at 56.

47 RUDOLF DOLZER & CHRISTOPH SCHREUER, PRINCIPLES OF INTERNATIONAL INVESTMENT LAW 224 (2008); ANTONIO R. PARRA, THE HISTORY OF ICSID 66–67 (2012).

48 Kenneth J. Vandevelde, *A Brief History of International Investment Agreements*, 12 U.C. DAVIS J. INT'L L. & POL'Y 157, 168–70 (2005).

49 Susan D. Franck, *The Legitimacy Crisis in Investment Treaty Arbitration: Privatizing Public International Law Through Inconsistent Decisions*, 73 Fordham L. Rev. 1521, 1625 n.16 (2005) ("The first stage involved Germany and Switzerland signing agreements with a variety of less developed countries in the early 1960s. The second stage occurred throughout the 1960s and into the 1970s when France, the United Kingdom, the Belgo-Luxembourg Economic Union, the Netherlands, and Norway involved themselves in the program. The final stage began in the late 1970s and continued into the early 1980s when Japan and the United States became increasingly involved.").

50 John F. Coyle, *The Treaty of Friendship, Commerce and Navigation in the Modern Era*, 51 Colum. J. Transnat'l L. 302, 327 (2013) ("Like the FCN treaty, the stated purpose of the

Accordingly, ISA only grew in popularity and use as the principal justifications for the compact remained in place: (1) a desire on the part of developing states to increase their ability to access foreign capital necessary for development on the part of capital-importing states; (2) a desire to reduce the diplomatic costs of protecting their nationals' capital on the part of capital-exporting states;[51] and (3) a desire for the protection of their capital from the expropriatory whims of developing nations on the part of foreign investors[52] independent of those investors ability to seek political solutions in the form of diplomatic protection.[53]

So long as ISA served the purposes of the original compact between capital-importing and capital-exporting states, its existence and legitimacy remained intact. As we will see in the following section, however, the rise of multilateral investment agreements involving multiple traditionally capital-exporting States ensured that the institution of ISA spread beyond the bilateral arrangements it was initially intended to service. Subjecting the judiciaries and regulatory decisions of traditionally capital-exporting states to the institution of ISA produced the challenges to the institutions legitimacy imperiling ISA's survival.

BIT was to protect the interests of U.S. nationals doing business overseas. Accordingly, State Department officials borrowed a great many provisions that had historically been a part of the FCN treaties in drafting this model agreement."); *see also* Franck, *supra* note 49 at 1525–26 ("In order to avoid the historical difficulties associated with "gunboat diplomacy," countries have promulgated treaties to promote foreign investment and instill confidence in the stability of the investment environment. This movement began with Treaties of Friendship, Commerce and Navigation, but soon moved beyond this as these treaties were limited commitments that did not have a forum for resolving disputes.").

51 Stephen M. Schwebel, Keynote Address: In Defence of Bilateral Investment Treaties, at 2, available at http://www.arbitration-icca.org/media/2/14169776244680/schwebel_in_defence_of_bits.pdf. ("[T]he displacement of gunboat diplomacy by international arbitration is a very real achievement."); Corn Products Int'l, Inc. v. Mexico, ICSID Case No. ARB(AF)/04/01, Decision on Responsibility, Sep. Op. Arbitrator Lowenfeld, para. 1 (Jan. 15, 2008) ("[T]he essential feature of investor-state arbitration, as it has developed since the ICSID Convention of 1965, … is that controversies between foreign investors and host states are insulated from political and diplomatic relations between states.").

52 For additional explanation of the ways in which diplomatic protection disadvantages foreign investors, *see* Puig & Shaffer, *supra* note 39 at 398–399.

53 Charles N. Brower & Sadie Blanchard, *What's in a Meme? The Truth about Investor-State Arbitration: Why It Need Not, and Must Not, Be Repossessed by States*, 52 Colum. J. Transnat'l L. 689, 757 (2014) ("Another way that investor-State arbitration has enhanced the international rule of law is that the grant of an enforceable right directly to the foreign investor decouples his ability to obtain redress for a wrong from his influence within his home state.").

3 *The Collapse of the Capital-Importing/Capital-Exporting Binary*

Towards the end of the 20th century, investors began to invoke arbitration provisions against traditionally-capital exporting states as the distinction between capital-importing and capital-exporting states blurred. This blurring of the distinction between capital-importing and capital-exporting states was a function of two key trends. First, states elected to include ISA provisions not only in bilateral investment agreements between traditionally capital-importing and traditionally capital-exporting states, but also in large multilateral agreements between a mix of countries in both groups. Indeed, even BITs between or free trade agreements amongst predominately capital-exporting countries included ISA provisions.

Second, the global dispersion of capital, partially facilitated by the first wave of bilateral investment treaties, meant that even traditionally capital-importing states now possessed nationals looking abroad for places to invest their capital. Accordingly, the rise of multilateral investment agreements involving multiple traditionally capital-exporting states, such as the North American Free Trade Agreement (including both Canada and the United States) and the proposed Trans-Pacific Partnership, inaugurated the second era of the institution of investor-state arbitration.[54] The compromise struck between capital-exporting and capital-importing states which sustained and justified the expansion of the institution of ISA throughout the latter part of the twentieth century was no longer sufficient to justify investors from, for example, Canada challenging the regulatory decisions of the United States' Environmental Protection Agency before independent arbitrators.

In *Loewen v. United States*, for example, the jury verdict rendered by a state court in the United States was challenged as a violation of the federal government's obligation to provide "fair and equitable treatment" to foreign investors.[55] The potential for subjecting the United States' judicial system to review by independent and private arbitrators raised significant political threats to the institution of ISA from one of the institution's strongest supporters: the United States. Similarly, the $15 billion NAFTA suit brought by TransCanada Corporation against the United States over the cancellation

54 Alvarez & Park, *supra* note 6 at 398 ("Until recently, the world of investment arbitration knew fairly clear lines between host and investor states. Nations such as Libya and Mexico were the respondent host states, while the United States and Canada were the countries of the investor claimants. Today, however, the United States and Canada under NAFTA have tasted the flavor of being respondent host states in investment arbitrations, with concomitant negative side-effects for economic self-governance.").

55 Loewen, ICSID Case No. ARB (AF)/98/3, Interim Award on Jurisdiction (Jan. 5, 2001), para. 2, http://www.naftaclaims.com.

of the Keystone XL pipeline for environmental reasons was only suspended pursuant to mutual agreement after the Trump Administration facilitated approvals for the pipeline. Had the pipeline's creation remained in question for environmental or other regulatory reasons, it is not difficult to imagine the political opposition to a $15 billion dollar payment to a foreign company to resolve a challenge to a regulatory decision made by the federal government should TransCanada Corporation have prevailed in arbitration.

While the traditionally capital-exporting states are no doubt subject to fewer investor-initiated disputes than capital-importing states, the presumption of legitimacy and fairness with which traditionally capital-exporting states view their own judiciaries and governmental institutions has led to the development of political challenges to the continued expansion of the institution of ISA.[56] Some traditionally capital-importing states have and continue to challenge the institution of ISA.[57] But the majority of capital-importing states have proven willing to acquiesce to the institution of ISA to enhance the accessibility of foreign direct investment.[58] Accordingly, the primary threat to ISA has emerged from the states that had previously supported the institution, or even imposed it on capital-importing states. Political movements from traditionally capital-exporting states suddenly subjected to investor-initiated disputes have produced the challenges endangering the survival of investor-state arbitration. The existence of ISA thus depends upon the willingness of traditionally capital-exporting states to advocate for the inclusion of the institution in future investment and trade agreements, rendering the emerging political challenges

---

56 *See, e.g.*, Anthea Roberts, *Triangular Treaties: The Extent and Limits of Investment Treaty Rights*, 56 Harv. Int'l L. J. 353, 360 (2015) (noting that "the interests of major states in the investment treaty system have started to converge" because "many states are increasingly becoming capital exporters (home states) as well as capital importers (host states) and thus are beginning to more closely approximate entities that find themselves in a situation analogous to Rawls' original position.").

57 Puig & Shaffer, *supra* note 39 at 365 ("In the last decade, countries have terminated BITs with ISDS clauses (such as Ecuador, Indonesia, and South Africa), withdrew from the ICSID Convention (notably, Bolivia, Ecuador, and Venezuela), threatened to leave it (including Argentina, El Salvador, and Nicaragua) …").

58 Reisman, *supra* note 2 at 62 ("First, the reaction is not being led by the governments of developing and capital-importing countries, from whom antipathy to foreign investment law's increasing application of high international standards to domestic governmental actions would usually have been expected. Although a few mineral-rich States have denounced some of their investment treaties, the vast majority of the developing countries continue to subscribe to arrangements that were forged to encourage cross-border direct foreign investment.")

from traditionally capital-exporting states to ISA an existential threat to the institution's survival.[59] The following section addresses these challenges.

Part 2: Contextualizing the Backlash against Investor-State Arbitration

In response to subjecting historically capital-exporting states to investor-initiated disputes, the twenty-first century challenges to investor-state arbitration contest both state-endorsed components of the grand bargain that the creation of the institution of investor-state arbitration embodied. Although these challenges have emerged from both traditionally capital-importing and traditionally capital-exporting states, the focus of this section rests on the political challenges arising from capital-exporting states. Because support for investor-state arbitration has always been tepid amongst capital-importing states, and those same states have treated the institution as a necessary cost of attaining investment and trade agreements with capital-exporting states, it is the political challenges in capital-exporting states that pose an existential threat to the institution of investor state arbitration. The challenges are twofold.

First, the rise of nationalism now challenges investor-state arbitration's stated purpose of enhancing the availability and decreasing the cost of foreign capital. At its most coherent, the nationalist right (and, to a lesser though still present extent, nationalist left) views capital as a scarce resource for which every nation competes, rendering capital-exporting state's support for investment protections such as ISA a mechanism for facilitating the loss of capital, and decreasing the power of the investor's home state vis-à-vis the foreign state in which the investment is made. We classify this challenge to ISA as emerging from the neo-mercantilist worldview of the nationalist right, as it refracts the historical mercantilism premised on a zero-sum competition between States to maximize exports while minimizing imports. As applied to capital investments, which are understood by the nationalist-right as wealth generating, the neo-mercantilist approach seeks to maximize the importation of foreign capital while minimizing the exportation domestic capital.

59 Brower & Blanchard, *supra* note 53 at 763 (describing a recent "movement of nationalistic opposition to foreign direct investment in a number of more developed states" apparent in "coercive attempts to regain control over previously privatized natural resources and nationalistic protectionism").

While the nationalist right in traditionally capital-exporting states may actively court foreign investment in their own state as a source of wealth enhancement, this worldview opposes the exportation of their own state's capital as the loss of the benefits of investment. Simultaneously, the nationalist and populist movements in traditionally capital-importing states oppose the importation of foreign capital on grounds similar to those advanced in the 1960s and 1970s: an opposition to foreign control of a state's resources as a form of neo-colonialism. Because investor-state arbitration facilitates the outflow of capital from capital-exporting states by providing protections and decreasing the risk of foreign investment, then, the neo-mercantilist nationalist right challenges the institution of ISA at least when adopted in agreements between traditionally capital-exporting and traditionally capital-importing states.

Second is the more consistent and more threatening challenge to the democratic legitimacy of the other state-endorsed component of the grand bargain: the resolution of investor-initiated disputes by independent, third party arbitrators.[60] According to this challenge to investor-state arbitration in its most direct form, arbitrators exert judicial or quasi-judicial power over a state's regulatory decisions, and only democratically-legitimated bodies may exercise of such power. Unlike national legislatures, judiciaries, or administrators, however, arbitrators lack the democratic legitimacy grounded in accountability to a democratic political body that justifies their exertion of state power, or so this challenge contends. Though this challenge recognizes the democratic legitimacy of the process through which the relevant states adopted the treaty

60 The burgeoning academic industry of work addressing what is pejoratively termed the "legitimacy crisis" in investor-state arbitration includes: Charles N. Brower, *A Crisis of Legitimacy*, Nat'l L.J. (7 Oct 2002); Charles H. Brower II, *Structure, Legitimacy, and NAFTA's Investment Chapter*, 36 Vand. J. Transnat'l L. 37 (2003); Charles N. Brower, Charles H. Brower II and Jeremy K. Sharpe, *The Coming Crisis in the Global Adjudication System*, 19 Arb. Int'l 415 (2003); Ari Afilalo, *Towards a Common Law of International Investment: How NAFTA Chapter 11 Panels Should Solve Their Legitimacy Crisis*, 17 Georgetown Int'l Envt'l L. Rev. 54 (2004); Ari Afilalo, *Meaning, Ambiguity and Legitimacy: Judicial (Re-)construction of NAFTA Chapter 11*, 25 Nw. J. Int'l L. & Bus. 279, 282 (2005); M. Sornarajah, "A Coming Crisis: Expansionary Trends in Investment Treaty Arbitration" in Karl P. Sauvant, ed., Appeals Mechanism in International Investment Disputes (2008) pp. 39–45; Gus Van Harten, Investment Treaty Arbitration and Public Law (Oxford 2007); Olivia Chung, *The Lopsided International Investment Law Regime and Its Effect on the Future of Investor-State Arbitration*, 47 Va. J. Int'l L. 953 (2007) (arguing that existing bilateral investment treaties strongly favor investors and that these inequalities will eventually lead to greater difficulties in enforcement of such treaties); Naveen Gurudevan, *An Evaluation of Current Legitimacy-based Objections to NAFTA's Chapter 11 Investment Dispute Resolution Process*, 6 San Diego Int'l L.J. 399 (2005).

authorizing the delegation of such authority to private arbitrators,[61] this challenge nonetheless contends that certain functions of government (including the de facto judicial power over a state's regulatory decisions at question in this challenge) simply may not be delegated to non-state actors.

Accordingly, both obligations that states accepted in the grand bargain—capital-exporting states' willingness (initially, enthusiasm) to permit the exportation of capital in exchange for the purportedly neutral and private resolution by arbitrators of disputes concerning that capital—are under attack. The sections that follow will explain in greater detail the nature and political origins of those attacks on the institution of investor-state arbitration. By detailing the political backlash against the fundamental premises of the grand bargain, we hope to illustrate the fundamental inadequacy of any attempt to tinker with the institution of investor-state arbitration. Modifying the process by which a tribunal arrives at its determinations, or even the standards against which such determinations are made, will do little to rebut challenges to ISA that oppose the institution's very purpose (the promotion of foreign investment) or the institution's very existence (as an independent and non-state method for resolving legal disputes).

1 *The Nationalist Return to Mercantilism*

The challenge to the institution of ISA posed by the rise of nationalism takes on numerous, often-inconsistent forms in both capital-exporting and capital-importing states. Regardless of the form or economic status of the state in question, however, the target of the nationalist challenge to ISA remains the same: the promotion of foreign direct investment. In capital-importing states, the nationalist challenge to ISA resembles the Marxist-inflected opposition to foreign control of a state's resources that emerged in newly-independent states following the collapse of the European empires after the Second World War. This nationalist challenge to foreign investment contends that a nation's resources should remain owned by its own nationals, whether in the form of express nationalization or, more commonly in the post-Cold War world, through ownership by a state's nationals in their private capacity.

Within traditionally capital-exporting states, the challenge posed by nationalism has expresses itself in two manifestations. The first manifestation of the nationalist challenge does not reject foreign investment (whether importing

61 Posner, *supra* note 12 at 813 ("The populist backlash against international law encompasses international law with impeccable democratic credentials like NAFTA and the WTO system, both of which were incorporated into domestic law by the president and Congress.").

or exporting), but instead seeks to manipulate the channels of that investment for political gain by maximizing foreign investment in its own state and minimizing the flow of capital out of its own state. We characterize this challenge as unprincipled, because it does not employ any internally consistent economic worldview, but instead merely seeks to exploit the levers of power for the enrichment of those advancing this world view. The unprincipled nature of this challenge is simple to refute theoretically, but requires a politically-sound worldview capable of defeating the self-enriching, would-be autocrats who adopt this approach.

The second manifestation of the nationalist challenge present in traditionally capital-importing states similarly does not reject outright foreign investment, but instead seeks to limit a state's exportation of capital. This challenge conceives of capital, and the wealth creation it provides, as a scare resource over which all states are in a zero-sum competition. Accordingly, a state should not provide any protections for its own nationals who invest abroad—and thereby deprive the state of the benefits of that investment—and instead create all incentives for the domestic investment of capital. The subsections below explore each challenge in turn.

1.1 The Populist Challenge to ISA in Capital-Importing States

In traditionally capital-importing states, the nationalist challenge to ISA invokes the initial objections to foreign direct investment following the collapse of the European empires after the Second World War: previously capital-importing states should not surrender control over the development of their own resources.[62] The contemporary populist challenge to ISA in traditionally capital importing states has generally emerged after arbitral tribunals ruled against the states in question, or even merely following the initiation of investor-state disputes.[63] The states on the losing end of numerous investor-initiated disputes, or a smaller number of costlier disputes, sought to renounce

62 *See, e.g.*, UN General Assembly's Declaration on the Establishment of a New International Economic Order. GA Resolution A/RES/S-6/3201 (1 May 1974) and its Charter of Economic Right and Duties of States (CERDS), GA Resolution A/Res/40/182 (17 December 1984). *See also* Puig & Shaffer, *supra* note 39 at 364 (explaining that newly independent and developing states sought to create an economic order "that recognized their sovereign ownership of their natural resources and championed the exclusive use of domestic law and institutions").

63 Malcolm Langford & Daniel Behn, *Managing Backlash: The Evolving Investment Treaty Arbitrator?*, European Journal of Int'l L. 6 (2016) ("Bolivia (2007), Venezuela (2009), and Ecuador (2012) denounced the ICSID Convention as a response to being sued under various IIAs; Ecuador and Bolivia terminated many of its BITs; and South Africa placed a moratorium on the signing of new IIAs pending an extensive policy review.").

their membership in ICSID, and terminate their investment agreements. These states include Bolivia, Venezuela, and Ecuador.[64] States that serve as both capital-exporting and capital-importing countries, such as South Africa, have attempted to terminate investment agreements with the states from which they traditionally import capital, while maintaining investment agreements providing ISA protections with states to which they traditionally export capital.[65]

Though the post-Second World War challenge to foreign direct investment sounded in Marxism and sought nationalization of a state's resources, the contemporary nationalist and populist challenge is not so ideologically unified. Some traditionally capital-importing states again seek nationalization of the state's resources from a Marxist perspective seeking state control over sources of wealth, but others instead seek merely for their own nationals to control the state's resources in their private capacity.[66] For example, while the populist

---

64 *Id.*

65 *See, e.g.*, Charles N. Brower & Jawad Ahmad, *Why the 'Demolition Derby' That Seeks to Destroy Investor-State Arbitration?*, 91 S. Cal. L. Rev. 1139, 1182 (2018) ("While South Africa has moved to terminate its BITs with Western European countries, such actions should not necessarily be interpreted as a broader revolt against investor-State arbitration. Thus far, no termination policy has been adopted in respect of South Africa's BITs currently in force with other African States including the South Africa-Zimbabwe BIT, the South Africa-Mauritius BIT, the South Africa-Nigeria BIT, the South Africa-Senegal BIT, and the SADC Investment Protocol.").

66 *See, e.g.*, Erik Voeten, *Populism and Backlashes against International Courts*, 18(2) Perspectives on Politics, 407–422 (2020) ("The backlash against investment arbitration serves as the most straightforward illustration. It is no coincidence that Latin America's left-wing populist governments, Bolivia, Ecuador, and Venezuela, are the ones who have ended their commitments to ICSID.85 Bolivia and Ecuador have even altered their constitutions to prohibit international investment arbitration. The opposition to ICSID was in part driven by costly adverse judgments but it was also ideological. In each country, there was pre-existing mobilization against neoliberalism and neoimperialism. These governments had been arguing for some time that foreign direct investment promotes imperialism and hinders the distribution of benefits from natural resources to the people. Venezuela left the Andean Community in 2006 objecting to bilateral free trade agreements that fellow member states Peru and Ecuador created free trade agreement with the United States. Chavez claimed that "it makes no sense for Venezuela to remain in the CAN, a body which serves only the elites and transnational companies and not our people, the Indians and the poor."); *See*, also, M. Sornarajah, *The Descent into Normlessness*, *in* EVOLUTION IN INVESTMENT TREATY LAW AND ARBITRATION 631, 640 (Chester Brown & Kate Miles eds., 2012) (arguing "that many States which have been at the wrong end of the stick have withdrawn or are contemplating withdrawal."). Puig & Shaffer, *supra* note 39 at 365 (explaining that, "[i]n the last decade, countries have terminated BITs with ISDS clauses (such as Ecuador, Indonesia, and South Africa), withdrew from the ICSID Convention (notably, Bolivia, Ecuador, and Venezuela)" or "threatened to leave it (including Argentina, El Salvador, and Nicaragua)").

challenge to ISA from traditionally capital-importing states in Latin-America has adopted left-wing, Marxist rhetoric that seeks nationalization and state-ownership of the country's resources, right-wing populist governments in the traditionally capital-importing states of Europe have employed a more xenophobic campaign opposing foreign—but not necessarily private—ownership of resources in the state. The right-wing populist government in Poland, for example, announced its intention to withdraw from all its investment agreements as part of the regime's broader backlash against review of government action.[67] Thus, despite the fact the nationalist challenge from traditionally capital-importing states to foreign direct investment was initially associated with the Marxist-left during the early Cold War, the reemergence of opposition to foreign direct investment owes much to the rise of both leftist and rightist populism in those states.[68]

Regardless of the precise political orientation of this challenge, the threat to the institution of investor-state arbitration pales in comparison to that posed by the nationalist right backlash in capital-exporting states, so long as capital-importing states continue to view foreign capital as a necessity. Given the imperatives for economic growth, particularly in states governed by regimes of dubious democratic legitimacy, and the role of foreign investment in promoting that growth, the nationalist backlash in capital-importing states is unlikely to constitute an existential threat to the institution of investor-state arbitration in the same way that the backlash in capital-exporting states may do so. Ecuador, for example, has recently attempted to renegotiate its cancelled investment agreements, even allowing for ISA protections for foreign investors in an effort to increase the availability of foreign capital despite significant distrust of ISA from previous unfavorable outcomes.[69] As the example of Ecuador

67 *Id.* at 24 (citing Orecki, Marcin. 2017. Bye-Bye BITs? Poland Reviews Its Investment Policy. *Kluwer Arbitration Blog*. Available at <http://kluwerarbitrationblog.com/2017/01/31/bye-bye-bits-poland-reviews-investment-policy/>. Accessed 23 June 2017.)

68 *See, e.g.*, Voeten, *supra* note 66 at Table 1 (noting India, Indonesia, Poland, Bolivia, Ecuador, and Venezuela have all exited or threatened to exit and or nullify the investor-state arbitration provisions of investment agreements). Voeten later classifies the leaders to initiate withdrawal from investor-state arbitration agreements as populist or not populist, *id.* at 421, and concludes that every withdrawal from an investor-state agreement involved a populist leader.

69 *See, e.g.*, Brower & Ahmad, *supra* note 66 at 1182 (explaining that one of the Latin American states to have renounced many of its investment agreements, Ecuador, "now is backpedaling," as "Ecuador's new Minister for Foreign Trade, Pablo Campana, has said: '[i]n order to secure private direct investment, we must have BITs,'" and "Ecuador has sent a proposal to fifteen countries inviting them to renegotiate the cancelled bilateral investment treaties").

demonstrates, if the traditionally capital-importing states remain politically motivated to require investor-state arbitration provisions in investment agreements, the capital-exporting states will have little choice but to acquiesce to the inclusion of such provisions. And at least with regard to bilateral investment agreements between capital-importing and capital-exporting states, the capital-exporting states continue to support the inclusion of ISA dispute settlement provisions.

1.2 The Unprincipled Challenge to ISA in Capital-Exporting States

In traditionally capital-exporting and states with both capital-exporting and capital-importing characteristics, the nationalist right has challenged investor-state arbitration in two ways. In its least principled manifestation, the nationalist right has not so much sought to limit foreign investment as it has sought to seize control of the political and civic institutions that regulate and facilitate foreign investment, and then manipulate that investment for their own political purposes. That manipulation of foreign investment may take the form of costly and largely symbolic handouts to a set of politically-connected investors capable of influencing the state to ensure their industries remain protected, or pure self-enrichment and crony-capitalism. Although the "new NAFTA," for example, purported to end the investor state arbitration mechanism, and in fact did so between for investments between the United States and Canada, the agreement did not fundamentally disturb the availability of investor state arbitration for investors from the United States in Mexico.[70] Indeed, although limiting the scope of economic sectors in which ISA would be available, the agreement expressly provided for ISA to resolve claims premised on either government contracts or the conduct of state-owned enterprises in a large number of industries most prominently involved in foreign investment disputes that end in ISA, including oil and gas, power generation, telecommunications, transportation, and infrastructure.[71] Very few foreign investors to

70 *See*, Article 14.2(4), Agreement between the United States of America, the United Mexican States, and Canada 7/1/20 ("For greater certainty, an investor may only submit a claim to arbitration under this Chapter as provided under Annex 14-C (Legacy Investment Claims and Pending Claims), Annex 14-D (Mexico-United States Investment Disputes), or Annex 14-E (Mexico-United States Investment Disputes Related to Covered Government Contracts).").

71 Annex 14-E-1(6)(b) clarifies that the "covered sectors" includes "activities with respect to oil and natural gas that a national authority of an Annex Party [the United States or Mexico] controls … the supply of power generation services to the public on behalf of an Annex Party, (iii) the supply of telecommunications services to the public on behalf of an Annex Party, (iv) the supply of transportation services to the public on behalf of an Annex Party, or (v) the ownership or management of roads, railways, bridges, or canals that

have invoked ISA provisions would fall outside this expansive carve-out, and the inclusion of the enumerated industries to ensure the continued availability of ISA for investors in those sectors was almost certainly a function of the political clout of investors operating in those industries.

The proposed Foxconn plant in the United States, heavily championed by then-President Trump, illustrates the danger of this unprincipled and inconsistent neo-mercantilist opposition to the free flow of foreign investment when it manifests in crony-capitalism. In this model for attracting foreign investments, states construct incentive packages to attract politically-connected foreign investors for the benefit of politically-connected domestic constituencies.[72] Despite discouraging the exportation of capital, the unprincipled nationalist right seeks the importation of foreign capital, viewed as a source of wealth creation that would otherwise flow to a competitor state. Accordingly, the nationalist right pursues foreign investment by putting together packages of costly incentives, tax breaks, and outright cash payments to incentivize particular investments that often benefit only a politically-connected subset of the capital-importing state. Thus, absent consistent and national implementation, the ad hoc creation of incentive packages to attain foreign investment lends itself to abuse and inefficiencies, whereby special protections are afforded to politically-connected foreign investors and granted to politically-connected locations.

This unprincipled critique of investor-state arbitration from the nationalist right reflects the nationalist right's broader attempt to distort the civic and political institutions of liberalism for the benefit of political allies. We define liberalism as the coupling of: (1) efforts to break down economic barriers

are not for the exclusive or predominant use and benefit of the government of an Annex Party."). *See also* Jack Caporal & William Alan Reinsch, "From NAFTA to USMCA: What's New and What's Next?," (October 3, 2018), available at: https://www.csis.org/analysis/nafta-usmca-whats-new-and-whats-next ("The investor-state dispute settlement provision (ISDS) of USMCA will cover investments in Mexico only in oil and gas, power generation services, telecommunication services, transportation services, and the management of ownership of infrastructure.").

72 *See, e.g.*, Dan Kaufman, "Did Scott Walker and Donald Trump Deal Away the Wisconsin Governor's Race to Foxconn?", THE NEW YORKER, (Nov. 3, 2018). Kaufman details how the incentive package model for attracting foreign investment led to President Trump incentivizing the construction of a factory in a state crucial to his electoral prospects and with an outsized influence on his administrative policy decisions given his Chief of Staff, for a foreign investor who attained that package by meeting personally with the President. The costs of the incentive package "include taxpayer subsidies to the company totally more than $4.5 billion, the largest subsidy for a foreign corporation in American history," with much of the subsidy provided "in direct cash payments from taxpayers."

between states with (2) a commitment to a civic order marked by rule of law, constrained conceptions of sovereignty, and promotion of private enterprise. The institution of investor-state arbitration reflects this conception of liberalism, pejoratively referred to as "globalism" by at least American elements of the nationalist right, by providing a mechanism to facilitate foreign direct investment and resolve disputes arising therefrom by recourse to a formalized legal dispute resolution mechanism rather than the economic, diplomatic, or even military pressures that capital-exporting states historically relied upon to protect the foreign investments of their nationals throughout much of history.

While paying lip-service to the democratic legitimacy concerns addressed in the section to follow, the unprincipled populist critique of ISA does not redress these concerns by either seeking meaningful restraints on the importation of foreign investment or a more democratically legitimate alternative mechanism for resolving disputes.[73] Instead, to the extent that this unprincipled challenge proposes an alternative to investor-state arbitration, it promises a return to diplomatic protection for the investments of the politically-connected as the primary means of protecting a state's own foreign investors. Under this model of investment protection, foreign states protect the investments of politically-connected investors, ultimately relying upon coercive tools of statecraft to extract concessions and protections from states in which the investments were made. In this way, the unprincipled populist and nationalist challenge to investor-state arbitration does not contain a principled rejection of investor-state arbitration, and instead seeks merely to redistribute the economic gains from increased foreign investment to politically connected groups. The unprincipled nature of this criticism, however, limits both the challenge's broader

73 At times, this unprincipled challenge to the institution of ISA has even adopted the left's concerns about the institution's democratic legitimacy, albeit couched in terms of sovereignty. *See, e.g.*, United States Trade Representative Robert Lighthizer's testimony at a House Ways and Means Hearing, available at: https://worldtradelaw.typepad.com/ielpblog/2018/03/brady-lighthizer-isds-exchange.html (asking "Why should a foreign national be able to come in and not only have the rights of Americans in the American court system but have more rights than Americans in the American court system?"). Lighthizer invokes the foreign investor requirements in investment agreements that are intended to ensure ISA does not provide an alternative mechanism for domestic investors to attain recovery for losses to their investments. Lighthizer's concerns are unwarranted; the institution of ISA provides a significantly riskier route to recovery than litigation in federal courts in the United States. No investor has prevailed in an investor-initiated dispute brought against the United States adjudicated before an arbitral tribunal, and arbitrators are likely even more swayed by the political implications of holding the United States liable in an investor-initiated dispute than would federal judges, who frequently rule against the United States in criminal and civil disputes.

political appeal and the capacity for the institution of investor-state arbitration to respond. Should this form of illiberalism nonetheless triumph, the institution of ISA—and, far more significantly, the global order upon which it rests—will not survive.

1.3 The Neo-Mercantilist Challenge to ISA in Capital-Exporting States

The more principled formulation of the nationalist challenge to the institution of ISA from within capital-exporting states adopts a neo-mercantilist opposition to the exportation of capital. We characterize this challenge as a "neo-mercantilist" one because it rests upon the assumption that nations are in competition for scarce capital, underpinning the challenge to ISA as a tool to facilitate the export of capital and therefore decreasing the capital and its attendant wealth-creating effects available to the investor's home state. To date, this approach has largely been rhetorical rather than substantive. For example, the United States Trade Representative who negotiated the revisions to NAFTA under President Trump, Robert Lighthizer, has framed the institution of ISA as a government subsidy for outsourcing,[74] and the renegotiated NAFTA agreement intends to phase out the availability of ISA for investments made by Canadian investors in the United States, and vice versa.[75]

Whether the application of a purportedly anti-outsourcing policy (the removal of investor-state arbitration as a mechanism available to investors) applied only to an agreement between two traditionally capital-exporting states, and not between the capital-importing and capital-exporting states, reflects a coherent or principled challenge to the exportation of capital is not clear. Even assuming that reducing incentives for the exportation of capital constitutes a desirable outcome, it would more effective to reduce incentives available to the investors of a traditionally capital-exporting state in an investment agreement with a traditionally capital-importing state, where the economics of outsourcing provide actual gains for the state's investors. That the United States, Canada, and Mexico sought and obtained the reverse in the renegotiated NAFTA suggests that accommodating business interests, which still resoundingly support the institution of investor-state arbitration,

---

74 Shawn Donnan, NAFTA: Bitter Differences over Nafta Break into the Open, FINANCIAL TIMES (Oct. 18, 2017), https://www.ft.com/content/058aa538-b387-11e7-a398-73d59db9e399 ("Mr Lighthizer ... said the [ISDS] system amounted to an unfair subsidy for businesses to invest overseas. 'Why is it my job to encourage people to invest in Mexico?'").

75 Caporal and Reinsch, *supra* note 71. ("The special arbitration mechanism contained in NAFTA that allowed investors to sue NAFTA countries for discriminatory actions will be phased out between the United States and Canada, and its coverage will be significantly trimmed for investors in Mexico.").

is a greater priority than meaningfully restricting the exportation of capital. Even the more ideologically coherent manifestation of neo-mercantilism amongst the nationalist right and left, then, may fail to present a principled objection to the institution of investor-state arbitration.

Nonetheless, this neo-mercantilism is at least rhetorically present in nationalist political movements, including in the United States. For example, the United States Trade Representative, in testimony before Congress, characterized ISA as equivalent to "political risk insurance" taken out by the federal government to protect companies outsourcing jobs to developing countries.[76] In this view, the inclusion of ISA in trade deals amounts to "underwriting [foreign] investment ... putting our finger on the scale, [] encouraging [investors] to move [their] plants [out of the country]."[77] That the same individuals then actively court the importation of capital through incentive packages does not necessarily mark as internally inconsistent the neo-mercantilist view of international trade espoused by the nationalist right, because each state in this worldview competes with other states for the importation of capital and the wealth-generation that follows.

Applied consistently, which it has not been, this challenge to investor-state arbitration would preclude a neo-mercantilist state from accepting investor-initiated arbitration provisions in investment agreements with states more likely to import capital than export capital. In other words, the United States would strongly oppose ISA dispute settlement provisions in bilateral investment agreements with states that the United States exports more capital to than it imports, while retaining the provisions in agreements with states from which the United States imports more capital than it exports. To the extent that investor-state arbitration provides a meaningful incentive to increase the availability of foreign investment, the hypothetically consistent neo-mercantilist state would willingly accept investor-state arbitration provisions in investment agreements reached with states more likely to export capital.

But because traditionally capital-exporting states generally have a stronger rule of private law governing investments, such provisions may not be necessary. This possibility provides the only explanation that would render consistent the United States' approach to ISA provisions in investment agreements such as the re-negotiated NAFTA, in which ISA remained available to US and Canadian investors in Mexico, a traditionally capital-importing state, but will be phased out for US and Canadian investors in either state. A more cynical and plausible explanation would suggest that the sole purpose of phasing

76 *Id.*
77 *Id.*

out the availability of ISA for Canadian investors in the US, while retaining the institution's availability between the US and Mexico, is solely to ensure that the United States itself faces as few investor-initiated disputes as possible. Because to date only one non-Canadian investor initiated an investment disputes against the US,[78] retaining ISA between Mexico and the US would maximize protections for American investors in Mexico while posing minimal risk to the United States. Regardless, the neo-mercantilist challenge to ISA does not justify the selective phasing out of ISA dispute settlement provisions that the United States has currently employed.

Despite the neo-mercantilist challenge's lack of concrete success in curtailing the availability of ISA to date, it nonetheless poses a significant challenge to the institution's survival. As explained in the section above, capital-importing states are generally resistant to the inclusion of ISA protections in investment agreements, both historically and in the present. The inclusion of such provisions thus depends upon traditionally capital-exporting states pushing strongly for the inclusion of such provisions to protect their own investors operating abroad. Any weakening of support for ISA within those capital-exporting states would then significantly decrease the likelihood that those provisions are included.

Because the neo-mercantilist challenge to ISA opposes the exportation of capital, an effective response then requires sufficient justification for the free flow of foreign investment and, assuming such a justification is economically possible, the more equitable distribution of the benefits derived from that free flow of investment so as to ensure adequate political support for the institution's existence. As we will explain in the Parts that follow, this is primarily a task of national rather than international politics, and will accordingly require national rather than international mobilization.

2 *Investor-State Arbitration's Democratic Legitimacy Deficiency*

This section addresses the most trenchant criticism of ISA: the institution's lack of democratic legitimacy. This challenge to ISA comes in a number of different forms; there indeed exists a cottage-industry of efforts to diagnose or refute ISA's "legitimacy crisis."[79] For our purposes, we categorize these challenges in two ways: the weaker and stronger formulations. Our characterization of the challenges as weaker and stronger does not necessarily refer to the relative merits of the challenges, but rather to the threat they pose to the institution of ISA.

78 *See* CANACAR v. United States of America, https://investmentpolicyhub.unctad.org/ISDS/Details/348.

79 *See* supra note 60.

In its weaker formulation, the democratic legitimacy challenge to the institution of ISA does not dispute the theoretical legitimacy of private (non-judicial) resolution of investor-initiated challenges to state actions. But, according to the weaker challenge, a number of problems with implementing the ISA process undermine the institution's legitimacy,[80] including: arbitral tribunals' inconsistent application of fixed standards,[81] partial private arbitrators more inclined to favor investors,[82] the revolving door of arbitrators and counsel,[83] bias against developing states,[84] lack of transparency,[85] and lack of appellate body.[86] We nonetheless categorize this disparate set of challenges to ISA's legitimacy as the weaker formulation of the legitimacy challenge because the object of criticism is not the process of arbitration itself, but rather the application of the process or the application of the standards governing the obligations a capital-importing state owes to foreign investors that arbitrators apply

80 José Alvarez & Gustavo Topalian, *The Paradoxical Argentina Cases*, 6 World Arb. & Mediation Rev. 491, 494 (2012).

81 Hueckel, Julia, *Rebalancing Legitimacy and Sovereignty in International Investment Agreements*, 61 EMORY LJ. 601, 606 (2012).

82 José Alvarez & Gustavo Topalian, *The Paradoxical Argentina Cases*, 6 World Arb. & Mediation Rev. 491, 494 (2012); *see also* Gus Van Harten, *Arbitrator Behaviour in Asymmetrical Adjudication: An Empirical Study of Investment Treaty Arbitration*, 50 Osgoode Hall Law Journal 211, 251 (2012) (arguing tribunals improperly favor investors when adjudicating an investor's rights in relation to a state's interest in regulating for the public interest); Jorge Viñuales, *Foreign Investment and the Environment in International Law* (Cambridge: Cambridge University Press, 2012) (arguing tribunals favor economic rights over public welfare objectives including environmental and public health protection). *Compare* Susan D. Franck, *The ICSID Effect? Considering Potential Variations in Arbitration Awards*, 51 VA. J. INT'L L. 825, 852 (2011) (noting that claimant's initiating investor-state disputes have a success rate of roughly forty percent) with Adam R. Pomeroy, *Penn Central After 35 Years: A Three Part Balancing Test or a One Strike Rule*, 22 FED CIR. B.J. 677, 698 (2012) (noting that in the United States, plaintiffs in eminent domain and 'regulatory takings' cases have a success rate of around four percent).

83 Malcom Langford, *et al.*, *The Revolving Door in International Investment Arbitration*, 20 Journal of Int'l Econ. Law 301 (2017) (noting that "closed nature of the [investor-state arbitral] community and its ability to engage in self-dealing" has "contributed to the so-called legitimacy crisis in investment arbitration.").

84 Thomas Schultz & Cedric Dupont, *Investment Arbitration: Promoting the Rule of Law or Over-Empowering Investors? A Quantitative Empirical Study*, 25 European Journal of International Law 1147 (2014) (arguing tribunals are more likely to rule against 'developing' host states).

85 Vaughan Lowe, Private Disputes and the Public Interest in International Law, in INTERNATIONAL LAW AND DISPUTE SETTLEMENT: NEW PROBLEMS AND TECHNIQUES 3, 10 (Duncan French et al. eds., 2010) (explaining that the United States now advocates for transparency in investor-state arbitration and public awards).

86 Hueckel, *supra* note 81 at 606.

during the process of ISA. In other words, the weaker formulation challenges the inputs to the institution of ISA: the way in which arbitrators selected, the arbitrators available to be selected, the standards of protection a state must provide a foreign investor, or other biases in the process of arbitration.

Though these criticisms expose important flaws in the institution's current form, we do not believe these challenges threaten to destroy the institution itself. Because ISA is a self-correcting institution as both the protections contained in investment agreements and the application of those protections can evolve over time, the weaker formulation poses minimal threat to the survival of the institution of ISA.

The same cannot be said for the stronger formulation of the legitimacy challenge. Articulated in this simplest and strongest formulation, the democratic legitimacy challenge to investor-state arbitration argues that privately constituted tribunals should not exert governmental or judicial power, which may be exercised only by the legitimate bodies of the state. So far, the institution of investor-state arbitration has been unable to refute this challenge, as the process for resolving disputes is the very object of the legitimacy challenge: the allocation of the right to private investors to sue sovereign states for violations of public law through a private system of adjudication.[87] Because this formulation refutes the legitimacy of the independent arbitral process itself, this formulation of the legitimacy challenge poses an existential threat to the institution of ISA, and cannot be resolved by mere modification to the institution's inputs, or so we will argue. The subsections that follow summarize these two challenges, and the inadequacy of the existing responses to the latter.

2.1 The Weaker Challenge

The weaker formulation of the challenge to the institution of ISA's legitimacy encompasses almost every criticism of ISA's application, from the standards that constitute the protections a host state must afford foreign investors to the method for selecting arbitrators. According to these challenges, nearly

87 *See* D. Behn, *Legitimacy, Evolution, and Growth in Investment Treaty Arbitration: Empirically Evaluating the State-of-the-Art*, 46(2) Georgetown Journal of International Law (2015) 363, 367 ("At its most fundamental level, the legitimacy debates in international investment treaty arbitration produce a critical perspective as to whether or not foreign investment disputes should be resolved by international arbitral tribunals at all. Some focus on the "international" part by claiming that foreign investment disputes are better resolved in the domestic context; others focus on the "arbitral" part by claiming that ad hoc, party-appointed arbitrators cannot adequately resolve public law disputes against sovereigns. These two meta-issues are related to dispute system design and provide the basis for many, if not all, the legitimacy challenges facing investment treaty arbitration to date.").

every criticism of ISA articulated by practitioners, scholars, and governmental officials contributes to the institution's purported legitimacy crisis. These problems vary from tribunals' inconsistent application of fixed standards,[88] arbitrator bias towards investors,[89] arbitrator financial incentives to favor investors to seek repeat appointments,[90] heightened scrutiny of regulatory actions taken by developing states in comparison to developed states,[91] lack of transparency accompanying the arbitral process,[92] the regulatory chill effect

88 Hueckel, *supra* note 81 at 606; Franck, *supra* note 49 at 1585 ("Coherence is another key element of legitimacy; it requires consistency of interpretation and application of rules in order to promote perceptions of fairness and justice."); Gabrielle Kaufmann-Kohler, 'Is Consistency a Myth?' in Emmanuel Gaillard and Yas Banifatemi (eds), Int'l Arbitration Inst, Precedent in International Arbitration (Juris Publishing, Inc 2008).

89 Alvarez & Topalian, *supra* note 82 at 494; *see also* Van Harten, *supra* note 82 at 251 (arguing tribunals improperly favor investors when adjudicating an investor's rights in relation to a state's interest in regulating for the public interest); Charles N. Brower & Stephan W. Schill, *Is Arbitration a Threat or a Boon to the Legitimacy of International Investment Law?*, 9 Chi. J. Int'l L. 471, 474–75 (2009) ("In other words, the criticism asserts that investment treaties and investment-treaty arbitration institutionalize a pro-investor bias that casts the legitimacy of the entire system of international investment law and arbitration into doubt."). Jorge Viñuales, *Foreign Investment and the Environment in International Law* (Cambridge: Cambridge University Press, 2012) (arguing tribunals favor economic rights over public welfare objectives including environmental and public health protection);

90 Brower & Schill, *supra* note 89 at 490 ("The second argument-the lack of permanent appointments-is the more serious criticism of investment-treaty arbitration. Arbitrators, the argument goes, earn their living by the fees they earn from appointments. Consequently, since they have an interest in being reappointed in future cases, they may be inclined to cater to the interests of those who will appoint them in the future. Arbitrators thus are viewed as having a financial stake in the outcome of the proceedings and therefore as not fully impartial and independent.").

91 Schultz & Dupont, *supra* note 84 (arguing tribunals are more likely to rule against 'developing' host states); Langford & Behn, *supra* note 63 at 6 ("In 2004 and 2004, the phrase 'legitimacy crisis' emerges in the academic scholarship for the first time and the crisis discourse extends clearly beyond its NAFTA origins. The awards rendered as a result of the Argentinian economic crisis of 2001 were particularly prominent (and numerous) and they produced a large amount of commentary. They continued to fuel the perception that investment treaty arbitration might favor foreign investors disproportionately and that [investment agreements] illegitimately restrict a state's regulatory autonomy in times of national emergency."). *But see* Susan D. Franck, *Development and Outcomes of Investment Treaty Arbitration*, 50 Harv. J. Int'l L. 435, 440 (2009) (concluding that "there are reasons to be cautiously optimistic about the system of investment treaty arbitration and its relationship with development variables.").

92 Vaughan Lowe, Private Disputes and the Public Interest in International Law, in INTERNATIONAL LAW AND DISPUTE SETTLEMENT: NEW PROBLEMS AND TECHNIQUES 3, 10 (Duncan French et al. eds., 2010) (explaining that the United States now advocates for transparency in investor-state arbitration and public awards).

that ISA may exert on democratically legitimate regulatory action,[93] and the unavailability of appeals to correct awards perceived to be illegitimate.[94]

These challenges are important to resolve for reasons internal to the institution of ISA, as they enhance the quality of arbitral process. Insofar as arbitrators, practitioners, and investment agreement drafters and negotiators should seek to maximize ISA's efficacy, we believe that this process occurs naturally in the evolution of arbitral case law interpreting investment agreement provisions,[95] and the evolution of those provisions themselves as investment agreements proliferate.[96] When the purportedly secretive nature of many investor-state arbitrations came under heavy criticism, for example, the United Nations Commission on international Trade Law (UNCITRAL) adopted Transparency Rules that require the publication of tribunal decisions and party submissions, open hearings, and submissions from non-parties.[97] The issuance of the Transparency Rules demonstrate the ways in which intergovernmental bodies enhance and supervise the arbitral process; because ISA exists pursuant

93 Kyla Tienhaara, Regulatory Chill and the Threat of Arbitration: A View from Political Science, in EVOLUTION IN INVESTMENT TREATY LAW AND ARBITRATION 606, 606 (Chester Brown & Kate Miles eds., 2011) (arguing that regulatory chill is an important problem "inadequately addressed and often prematurely dismissed by legal scholars").

94 Franck, *supra* note 49 at 1625 ("The ultimate utility of the system, however, will not be fully realized until an appellate court is created which permits correction of legal errors, which might otherwise inappropriately bankrupt developing nations, stifle legitimate regulatory activity, or deprive investors of their legitimate expectations.").

95 Tai-Heng Cheng, *Precedent and Control in Investment Treaty Arbitration*, 30 Ford. J. Int'l L. 1014, 1016 (2009) (arguing "there is an informal, but powerful, system of precedent that constrains arbitrators to account for prior published awards and to stabilize international investment law.").

96 *See, e.g.*, Alexander W. Resar, *The Evolution of Investor-State Arbitration in the Trans-Pacific Partnership Agreement*, 34 Berkeley J. Int'l L. 159, 162–63 (2016) (arguing "the TPP continues the largely responsive evolution in international investment treaties and agreements by examining the TPP's departures from the United States' most recent investment treaties and agreements in light of the arbitral decisions driving those changes."); Brower & Schill, *supra* note 89 at 494–95 ("Certainly, all contracting parties can get together and formally change an investment treaty or agree by other binding means on the interpretation to be given to certain investor rights. Similarly, the contracting parties can establish treaty organs, like NAFTA's Free Trade Commission, that are empowered to issue such interpretations and thereby steer investment tribunals into directions that are in tune with the states parties' intentions.").

97 Press Release, United Nations Information Service, UNCITRAL Adopts Transparency Rules for Treaty-Based Investor-State Arbitration and Amends the UNCITRAL Arbitration Rules (Dec. 18, 2013), available at http://www.unis.unvienna.org/unis/pressrels/2013/unisl186.html; UNCITRAL Rules on Transparency in Treaty-based Investor-State Arbitration, UNCTIRAL (Jan. 2014), available at http://www.uncitral.org/pdf/english/texts/arbitration/rules-on-transparency/pre-release-UNCITRAL-Rules-on-Transparency.pdf.

to agreements between states, states may always modify the arbitral process by adopting and implementing such rules so long as the underlying desire to retain ISA as a mechanism for resolving disputes remains.

Similarly, with regard to the evolution in arbitral case law to refine the standards that arbitrators employ to assess whether a state properly protected a foreign investment, recent empirical studies demonstrate that "arbitrators are conditionally reflexive" and "sensitive to both negative and positive signals" from particularly "vocal, influential and developed states."[98] Although the empirical analysis shows that arbitrators are more responsive to the concerns of a particular subset of developed states—perhaps accounting, at least in part, for the fact that the United States has never lost an investment dispute as the respondent state—,[99] arbitrators respond to criticisms that ISA is overly-investor friendly or overly-state friendly and modulate their behavior accordingly so as to preserve the legitimacy of the institution of ISA.

For example, when early arbitral tribunals came under criticism for failing to consider a state's "right to regulate," later tribunals began to make "good faith efforts to take seriously the state's 'right to regulate.'"[100] Thus, "since around the mid-2000s, ISDS decisions increasingly recognize that fairness should not be viewed in one-sided terms, focusing only on the foreign investor, given that the state has a responsibility to balance other welfare goals with the protection of

98 Langford & Behn, *supra* note 63 at 11–12 (explaining that arbitrators, as members invested in the institution of ISA, respond to state and public pressure). Curiously, the "revolving door" that critics of ISA argue undermines the institution's legitimacy may accentuate this responsiveness, as it ensures personal investment on behalf of arbitrators in the institution's survival.

99 *Id.* ("On one hand, we have shown that the system has adjusted considerably since its infancy. Claimant-investor success rates have fallen dramatically and hover around 40% today. This is certainly much lower than the comparable figure of 90%-plus for applicant states in WTO litigation. On the other hand, we have found a clear asymmetry in the distribution of the reflexive gains for states. It is developed states that are the beneficiaries of the large drop in claimant-investor success rates; less developed states have only registered marginal benefits.").

100 Alec Stone Sweet & Florian Grisel, The Evolution of International Arbitration: Judicialization, Governance, Legitimacy 190 (2017) ("in the vast majority of awards, tribunals made good faith efforts to take seriously the state's 'right to regulate'"). *See also* Alec Stone Sweet, Michael Yunsuck Chung & Adam Saltzman, *Arbitral Lawmaking and State Power: An Empirical Analysis of Investment Arbitration*, 7 J. INT'L DISP. SETTLEMENT 1, 16–17 (2017) ("As tribunals from Saluka forward have made clear, investors cannot expect regulatory arrangements to be frozen."); Suzanne A. Spears, *The Quest for Policy Space in a New Generation of International Investment Agreements*, 13 J. INT'L ECON. L. 1037, 1071 (2010) (explaining that tribunals presiding over investor-initiated challenges to a state regulation engage in a "balancing process" that requires the tribunal "make value judgments" balancing the state's right to regulate against the investor's legitimate expectations).

investment."[101] Instead, arbitrators began to consider whether a state's treatment of a foreign investment was instead motivated by a legitimate regulatory concern for the welfare of its population and treated the foreign investment no differently than domestic investors operating in the same commercial space. This evolution demonstrates that even if it were only possible for arbitrators to continue enforcing the same protections included in already-existing investment agreements, there exists strong evidence to suggest that the institution of ISA would be capable of self-correcting to the extent necessary to mollify criticisms of bias against states claims that arbitrators misapply the protections that should be afforded to foreign investors.

However, such informal self-correction may not even be necessary to ensure the continued evolution of the enforcement of the protections contained in investment agreements. Negotiators of investment agreements must respond to public political pressure on the inclusion or exclusion of certain provisions even if arbitrators alone were unwilling to modify their behavior in response to public pressures, and processes for ensuring arbitrator neutrality exist.[102] If, for example, arbitrators repeatedly interpret the fair and equitable treatment provisions contained in an investment agreement in a manner that the states party to the treaty consider problematic, the states may either issue guidance governing the interpretation of the provisions in question or renegotiate the investment agreements. As multilateral investment agreements cover an increasing segment of the global economy, the protections contained in investment agreements will only become increasingly standardized and harmonized, thereby providing a mechanism for the reconsideration of particularly problematic provisions.[103] In this way, newer multilateral investment agreements such as the Trans-Pacific Partnership provide a way to modernize and revise the protections afforded to investors across a broader set of interstate relationships.

Thus, although the weaker challenge to the legitimacy of ISA invokes problems that range from the institution's lack of transparency to the inconsistent

---

101 Puig & Shaffer, *supra* note 39 at 370.

102 Brower & Schill, *supra* note 89 at 491 (arguing appointment processes ensure arbitrator neutrality because of formal mechanisms, such as party challenges to an arbitrator's nomination and public scrutiny, and informal mechanisms, such as reputational costs).

103 Stephan Schill, *Multilateralizing Investment Treaties through Most-Favored-Nation Clauses*, 27 BERKELY J. INT'L L. 496, 561 (2009) ("Seeking the most favorable protection offered by the BITs of a specific host State is therefore not a shopping for unwarranted advantages, but the core objective of MFN clauses.... application of MFN clauses [to matters of jurisdiction] harmonizes compliance procedures for the host State's obligations under investment treaties.").

interpretation and application of provisions, the institution of ISA appears fully capable of evolution and self-correction.[104] Whether through informal processes including the refinement of arbitral case law and issuance of guidance by intergovernmental bodies or formal processes such as the renegotiation of investment agreements, the institution of ISA responds and evolves in response to criticism, so long as that criticism does not challenge the fundamental characteristics of ISA.

2.2 The Stronger Challenge

In its strongest formulation, the democratic legitimacy challenge to ISA questions the right granted to investors by investor-state arbitration provisions to resolve disputes arising from foreign investments before *private* arbitrators. In short, the democratic legitimacy challenge contends that private arbitrators lack the democratic legitimacy[105] necessary to exercise judicial power or governmental authority over a state's regulatory decisions.[106] By democratic legitimacy, we largely refer to what Professor Stephan Schill termed the "public law challenge" to international investment law, relating "to the observation that investment treaty arbitration restricts governmental action, and therefore concerns questions of public law, without relying on a dispute settlement mechanism that conforms to core public law values, including democracy,

---

104 *See, e.g.*, International Bar Association Report, Consistency Efficiency and Transparency in Investment Treaty Arbitration (Nov. 2018) (explaining the importance of fostering consistency, efficiency, and transparency in investment treaty arbitration to enhance the legitimacy of the institution); Brower & Schill, *supra* note 89 at 473 ("While some of these problems, in particular unpredictability and incoherence in investor-state dispute settlement, are considerable and in need of serious attention, arguably a solution will come with the passage of time. Increasing dispute-settlement procedures and doctrinal efforts promise to prove that concepts relating to investors' rights, such as fair and equitable treatment and indirect expropriation, are not as vague and indeterminate as some argue.").

105 We emphasize democratic legitimacy when addressing the legitimacy challenge to ISA, though we recognize other forms of legitimacy exist. Max Weber identified three sources of legitimacy, for example: tradition, charismatic leadership, or bureaucratic rationality. *See* Max Weber, Economy and Society: An Outline of Interpretive Sociology (Guenther Roth and Claus Wittich eds., 1968) (cited in Kingsbury & Schill, *supra* note 11 at 41). ISA cannot claim legitimacy through tradition nor charismatic leadership, requiring the institution to derive any Weberian legitimacy through rationality. *Id.* In democratic states who have historically driven the expansion of ISA, however, the institution requires democratic legitimization, hence our focus in this chapter on democratic legitimacy.

106 Brower & Schill, *supra* note 89 at 489 ("Critics argue that arbitration, as compared to dispute resolution in courts, is unsuitable for such public law disputes because arbitrators are privately contracted by the parties to specific disputes and do not hold, like tenured judges, a public office.").

equal treatment, separation of powers, legal certainty and predictability, or in other words, the rule of law."[107] Though states could always elect to pay future awards to similarly situated investors, a tribunal that determines a state's sovereign actions violates that state's obligations under an investment agreement functionally requires the state to change the decision for future similarly situated parties.[108] In this way, ISA enables private arbitrators to fundamentally alter a state's legal order, requiring a state to treat foreign investors differently than it otherwise would.

As an initial matter, there exists little doubt that tribunals presiding over investor-initiated disputes exercise governmental authority.[109] Because ISA tribunals resolve questions of public law such as the propriety of a state's regulatory choices under both international standards of treatment for foreign investors[110] and, most controversially, the state's own law,[111] they provide a binding rule of decision on the state. Paradoxically, the transition from early ISA tribunals, which neglected regulatory concerns in their single-minded efforts to enforce an investor's rights under an investment agreement, to modern ISA tribunals that consider a state's "right to regulate" increasingly required arbitral

107 Stephan W. Schill, *International Investment Law's Legitimacy*, 52 Va. J. Int'l L. 57, 67 (2011) (citing DAVID SCHNEIDERMAN, CONSTITUTIONALIZING ECONOMIC GLOBALIZATION: INVESTMENT RULES AND DEMOCRACY'S PROMISE 225 (2008) (arguing the institution of ISA "destabilize[s] the functioning of democratic processes, represented by other constitutional rules.").

108 Julian Arato, *Corporations as Lawmakers*, 56 HARV. INT'L L. J. 229, 231 (2015) (ISDS enables corporations "to create norms of international law—norms that bear a particular kind of relationship of priority to the state party's domestic legal order.").

109 Kingsbury & Schill, *supra* note 11 at 40 ("Whereas investment treaty arbitration faces legitimacy demands stemming from the fact that investment tribunals exercise control over the host State's conduct which operates in a public rather than a private sphere, commercial arbitration cases ordinarily are significant only for the disputing parties and their stakeholders, although on occasion these cases can have some precedential and even systemic implications ...").

110 *See, e.g.*, NAFTA, art. 1105(1) (requiring host states "accord to investments of investors of another Party treatment in accordance with international law, including fair and equitable treatment and full protection and security.").

111 *See* Cory Adkins & David S. Grewal, *Democracy and Legitimacy in Investor-State Arbitration*, 126 Yale L. J. FORUM (2016) ("By making a constitutional argument, TransCanada seeks to focus the tribunal on an exercise of constitutional interpretation, rather than on the State Department's broad and well-known power to reject permits inconsistent with the "national interest," or on the obvious risk that the pipeline would be rejected on other grounds. The use of ad hoc tribunals to judge constitutional matters appears to be the unfortunate next step in an increasingly intrusive jurisprudence of investment arbitration.").

awards to openly resolve questions of public law.[112] But the mere fact that ISA tribunals must address questions of public international law (or domestic law, in some circumstances) would be unlikely to trigger the legitimacy crisis ISA currently faces.

However, the implications for both investors and states of an arbitral decision are significant. In applying international law to a state's regulatory decisions, tribunals exert de facto judicial power over the implementation and application of sovereign state's actions. The state's actions challenged in ISA have been arrived at and implemented through the political processes of the state actor. In other words, the government action that arbitrators must assess has been reached through the host state's judicial, legislative, or regulatory processes, and would otherwise only be challengeable through those same processes. Although any particular tribunal exercises jurisdiction over only the sole dispute for which it was constituted, the widespread implications of a tribunal's award are readily apparent. A respondent state subject to an adverse award would face a decision to either make significant payments[113] to multiple similarly-situated investors, or to modify/repeal the challenged state action.

112 Puig & Shaffer, *supra* note 39 at 370 ("However, since around the mid-2000s, ISDS decisions increasingly recognize that fairness should not be viewed in one-sided terms focusing only on the foreign investor, given that the state has a responsibility to balance other welfare goals with the protection of investment") (citing, inter alia, STONE SWEET & GRISEL, *supra* note 100 at 190 ("[I]n the vast majority of awards, tribunals made good faith efforts to take seriously the state's 'right to regulate'").

113 There is no doubt that the amounts sought and awards issued by investor-state arbitral tribunals are significant. *See* Michael D. Goldhaber, Big Arbitrations, Focus Eur., Summer 2003, at 22 available at http://www.americanlawyer.com/focuseurope/bigarbitrations.html. The amounts sought include the following: (1) the "Czech TV Debacle" where the Czech Republic was sued for over U.S. $500 million; (2) the "Argentine Currency Crisis Claims" where the Republic of Argentina was sued for "billions of dollars"; (3) the "Lebanese Mobile Phone Fight" where U.S. $1.05 billion was disputed in a case involving the Republic of Lebanon; (4) the "Czech-Slovak Bank Battle" where the Slovak Republic was sued for U.S. $1 billion in damages; (5) the "Japanese-Czech Banking Battle" where a U.S. $1 billion claim was made against the Czech Republic; (6) the "Port Services Disputes" where claims are being brought claiming that the Islamic Republic of Pakistan owes approximately U.S. $350 million and the Republic of Philippines owes U.S. $120 million; (7) the "Building Bridges in Pakistan" where a claim for U.S. $450 million was made against the Islamic Republic of Pakistan; (8) the "Turkish Power Plant Joint Venture" where the Republic of Turkey is being sued for U.S. $300 million; (9) the "Argentine Water Dispute" alleging the Republic of Argentina owes U.S. $300 million; (10) the "Egyptian Textile Business Dispute" where the Arab Republic of Egypt is being sued for U.S. $250 million; and (11) the "Oil Contract Bidding Dispute" where a U.S. $200 million claim was brought against the Republic of Trinidad and Tobago. Especially for smaller states, awards in this amount may implicate significant percentages of the state's budget.

Because most investment agreements contain transparency provisions that mandate the publication of awards, other investors (and other states subject to similar investment agreements and considering similar regulatory decisions) would be aware of the existing challenges.[114] Accordingly, the sovereign power exerted by arbitral tribunals exceeds in its global scope even that exerted by a state's judiciaries in scope of impact, potentially implicating not only claims brought by investors against that host state, but also claims brought by investors against other states party and non-party to the given investment agreement. The creation of a permanent arbitral court to preside over investor-initiated disputes would be unlikely to curtail the widespread implications of any particular arbitral tribunal's interpretation of a given provision or principle, and would likely only enhance the scope of the tribunal's power.[115]

Additionally, a recent trend in arbitral tribunal's interpretation of minimum standard of treatment provisions contained in most investment agreements permits an investor to challenge a state's alleged violation of not only principles of international law, but the state's own law before private arbitrators.[116] The potential for arbitral tribunals to interpret and apply a state's own law by holding, for example, that a regulatory agency's potentially incorrect application of the host state's own law frustrated an investor's reasonable expectations,[117] uniquely emphasizes the strength of the democratic legitimacy challenge to the institution of ISA, because the private arbitral tribunal displaces the state's

114 *See* David Schneiderman, *NAFTA's Takings Rule: American Constitutionalism Comes to Canada*, 46 U. TORONTO L. J. 499, 503 (1996) (arguing that "NAFTA has altered significantly the constitutional make-up of the Canadian state").

115 Brower & Ahmad, *supra* note 65 at 1155 ("Japan views the proposed permanent court as "a 'world legislator' being in a position to decide highly sensitive and important issues without any accountability.'").

116 *See, e.g.*, Clayton v. Government of Canada, Award on Jurisdiction and Liability, Case No. 2009-04, ¶¶ 601–602 (Perm. Ct. Arb. 2015), http://www.pcacases.com/web/send Attach/1287.

117 *See, e.g.*, *id.* at ¶¶ 601–602 (Perm. Ct. Arb. 2015), http://www.pcacases.com/web/send Attach/1287 (holding, at least in some readings, that Canada violated the minimum standard of treatment provisions in NAFTA by arguably violating its own law in the failure to assess mitigation efforts in the Canadian equivalent to an environmental impact statement assessing a project's environmental consequences); TransCanada Keystone Pipeline, LP v. John Kerry, Complaint, Case 4:16-cv-00036 (S.D. Tex. filed Jan. 6, 2016) (likely previewing the arguments TransCanada would have made in an investor-initiated challenge to the United States' determination, eventually reversed following the 2016 Presidential election, not to grant an environmental permit to the Keystone XL pipeline between Canada and the United States).

judiciary as the final judge of the state's own law.[118] In other words, arbitral tribunals can in certain circumstances displace national judiciaries as the bodies that determine what a state's own laws mean, and how they may be properly implemented.

Moreover, in certain circumstances foreign investors may even be able to not only displace a state judiciary's understanding or application of that state's own law, but even to challenge that application or understanding. Prohibitions on the denial of justice, a provision contained in most investment agreements, provide one potential mechanism for private arbitrators to review a state's application of its own law. Because parties frequently require tribunals to apply the denial of justice standard when assessing a host state's judicial treatment of an investor, tribunals may review the host state's judiciary's application of its own law. For critics of ISA who argue that private arbitrators should not be able to exercise appellate power over a state judiciary, this review constitutes a troubling occurrence in light of the presumption that a state's own judiciary may exercise final interpretive power over the meaning and application of its own law.[119]

Even if private arbitral tribunals may legitimately interpret international legal standards, their capacity to legitimately interpret a state's obligations under its own law remains exceptionally difficult to legitimate. Arbitrators almost always do not owe any legal obligations to the state responsible for creating and applying the law that the arbitrators may interpret and apply, and are thus unaccountable for the interpretations and applications of a state's domestic law that their awards promulgate.[120] Though similar criticisms may, and have been, posed of judicial review writ large, the methods of democratically legitimizing judicial review are inapplicable to the institution of investor state arbitration.[121] The institution of ISA protects no political rights, for

---

118 *See, e.g.*, Michael D. Goldhaber, *The Rise of Arbitral Power Over Domestic Courts*, 1 Stan. J. of Complex Lit. 373, 416 (2013) (arguing that the "rise of arbitral power over domestic courts reinforces the need for arbitral institutions with judicial levels of legitimacy").

119 *See Id.* at 383 (explaining that "a party with means that believes it has been denied justice in a domestic court system will inevitably pursue a cause of action in another forum aimed at the restoration of justice").

120 Yackee, *supra* note 45 at 1610–11 (explaining that investor-state arbitral "decision-making has been placed primarily in the hands of an exceedingly small pool of super-elite, like-minded international lawyers who operate largely divorced from any local political process").

121 *See, e.g.*, Samuel Freeman, *Constitutional Democracy and Legitimacy of Judicial Review*, 9 L. and Phil. 327 (1990) (explaining that judicial review preserves the equal exercise of political rights).

example, and serves no broader democratic purpose to justify review of otherwise democratically legitimate state action.

Indeed, even the European Court of Justice, itself subject to similar legitimization challenges as a supranational governmental body, has adopted elements of the democratic-legitimacy critique of ISA when effectively eliminating the ISA provisions in intra-European Union BUTs. In *Achmea*, the European Court of Justice held that arbitral tribunals were inappropriate bodies to conclusively resolve questions of European Union law, because at least when constituted on an ad hoc basis, such tribunals are insufficiently grounded within the national judiciaries approved by the European Court of Justice.[122]

Accordingly, the democratic legitimacy challenge to ISA's exercise of judicial power presents a significant obstacle for the institution to overcome, and this challenge would retain at least some of its force even if arbitral tribunals uniformly adopted the most state-friendly interpretation of substantive provisions possible.[123] The subsection below addresses the existing attempts to defend the democratic legitimacy of ISA.

2.3 The Inadequacy of Existing Attempts to Legitimate ISA

In defense of the institution of investor-state arbitration, responses to the legitimacy challenge have emerged. These responses, however, have largely failed to refute the fundamental challenge to the democratic legitimacy of private arbitrators exercising governmental authority over a state's regulatory, judicial, or legislative decisions.

First, an initial defense of the institution of investor-state arbitration denies the public law nature of the arbitral tribunal's authority, arguing that arbitral tribunals presiding over investor-initiated suits award only compensation due to an investor for a state's violation of its treaty obligations. And because the only remedy an ISA tribunal can award is monetary damages, according to this defense, the tribunal does not necessarily preclude a state from pursuing whatever actions it wishes and merely entitles a foreign investor implicated by those actions to the compensation the state agreed to provide in the underlying investment agreement. This defense takes too narrow a view of the implications of an arbitral award, and denies the significant public law components of any arbitral award that assesses the legality of governmental action

---

122 *See, generally*, Janssen & Wahnschaffe, *supra* note 7.

123 Yackee, *supra* note 45 at 1610 ("If the modern BIT-based system of international investment law has a fundamental problem, the problem principally lies in the system's universalistic claims and pretensions, rather than in the occasional set of inconsistent arbitral decisions that other scholars have identified as the primary source of a crisis of legitimacy.").

under an international agreement to which the state acceded. Though any particular tribunal exercises jurisdiction only over the investor that initiated the dispute and the respondent state, tribunals' decisions interpreting and applying principles of international law implicate a wide range of actors not party to the dispute. Specifically, even without a system of binding precedent in investment treaty arbitration,[124] a tribunal's interpretation and application of a given provision provides persuasive authority for tribunals presiding over similarly situated investors.[125] In other words, to the extent that an investor successfully challenges an entire regulatory or legislative decision, other foreign investors also subject to that government action will certainly initiate similar challenges. Because the costs of defending such suits, and then paying awards, are significant, arbitral tribunals will exert de facto judicial power over the implementation and application of a host state's regulatory decisions.

Such concerns are plausible even if most states have avoided defending such "pile-on" investment claims to date. Australia, for example, only recently prevailed in a long-running dispute initiated by Philip Morris over a public health measure that the tobacco company considered expropriatory.[126] Should Philip Morris have prevailed, similarly situated tobacco companies would no doubt have brought identical claims until Australia modified or repealed the legislation. Nor are these concerns of repetitive challenges to state action purely hypothetical. Spain, for example, has faced a number of claims pertaining to its retraction following the 2008 financial crisis of certain investment incentives for renewable energy.[127] And, most famously, numerous foreign investors brought claims against Argentina arising from the government's response to the 2001–2003 Argentine financial crisis.[128]

---

124 Cheng, *supra* note 95 at 1016 (arguing "there is an informal, but powerful, system of precedent that constrains arbitrators to account for prior published awards and to stabilize international investment law").

125 Kingsbury & Schill, *supra* note 11 at 43–44.

126 Phillip Morris Asia Ltd. v. Australia, Case No. 2012–12, Award on Jurisdiction and Admissibility (Perm. Ct. Arb. 2015), http://www.italaw.com/sites/default/files/case-documents/italaw7303_0.pdf [http://perma.cc/Y4TX-VQR4]. The decision will be published pending redaction of confidential information.

127 *See, e.g.*, Isabella Reynoso, "Spain's Renewable Energy Saga: Lessons for international investment law and sustainable development," Investment Treaty News: International Institute for Sustainable Development (June 27, 2019), *available at*: https://www.iisd.org/itn/en/2019/06/27/spains-renewable-energy-saga-lessons-for-international-investment-law-and-sustainable-development-isabella-reynoso/.

128 *See* Gebhard Bucheler, Proportionality in Investor-State Arbitration, Oxford University Press: 2015, at Ch. 2, Investor-State Arbitration and the Argentine Cases.

Moreover, no single investment agreement exists in a vacuum; most international investment agreements grant investors similar protections; if the language is not identical, than at the very least the principles of international law invoked by particular provisions in investment agreements are shared between treaties. Accordingly, one tribunal's interpretation of the fair and equitable treatment standard under NAFTA in an investment dispute between an investor from Canada and in Mexico may implicate another tribunal's understanding of that same standard under the ECT between an investor from the Netherlands and in Poland.[129] In this way, international investment law differs significantly from the international commercial law model of ad hoc arbitration, and requires distinct justification with regards to the public law implications of ISA awards.[130]

And most significantly, the amount of damages awarded may be so significant as to dissuade states from pursuing certain regulatory outcomes even if only one investor may be implicated.[131] Investors initiating ISA proceedings frequently seek awards in the hundreds of millions or even billions, and awards of such magnitude may constitute a sizeable portion of a smaller state's yearly budget. And particularly large awards may create significant repercussions for even large economies were they to be paid. There can be little doubt, then, that ISA tribunals wield significant power over the actions of states that accede to agreements containing ISA dispute settlement provisions.

---

129 Kingsbury & Schill, *supra* note 11 at 43–44 (explaining that "a tribunal's decision on how to interpret and apply one of these open-ended provisions can have implications for non-participants, including dozens of other States and innumerable specific investments around the world, because identical or similar standards are obligatory in virtually every investment treaty relationship. The interpretation of such a provision by arbitral tribunals potentially shapes the future behavior of States and their legislatures and agencies, as well as the expectations and choices of investors and perhaps of other actors affected by investment-related issues.").

130 Schill, *supra* note 107 at 76 ("Because one of the disputing parties is not a private commercial actor, investment treaty awards are more likely to affect the host state's population directly, as the state, in order to comply with its international obligations, must adapt its behavior in order to avoid liability—for example, by allowing higher tariffs for basic utilities even if this cuts off access to that utility for a portion of the population, by permitting the use of harmful substances, or by repealing general regulatory policies. Investment treaty obligations and decisions by arbitral tribunals on such matters may thus directly affect the social fabric of the host state.").

131 *See* Kyla Tienhaara, Regulatory Chill and the Threat of Arbitration: A View from Political Science, in EVOLUTION IN INVESTMENT TREATY LAW AND ARBITRATION 606, 606 (Chester Brown & Kate Miles eds., 2011) (discussing the regulatory chill effect of arbitral awards that discourage states from regulating certain industries when the states understand that those regulations will be subject to investor-initiated challenges).

A stronger attempt to refute the legitimacy challenge argues that the treaty mechanism through which states create the possibility for investor-state arbitration constitutes a democratically legitimate delegation of sovereign power to private actors.[132] In other words, a state's negotiation of and entrance into an investment treaty or free trade agreement is a democratically legitimate sovereign action through which each state party acquiesces to limitations on the exercise of its regulatory powers, as determined by private investment tribunals.[133] The Honorable Charles Brower and Stephan Schill concisely advance this defense: "the consent to arbitration in investment treaties is itself a sovereign act of the state. Consequently, the basis of the arbitrators' authority in investment-treaty cases is founded in a public office which is conferred upon them based on international treaties. This counters the argument that public disputes under investment treaties are subjected to privatized dispute settlement."[134]

While acknowledging the democratic input required to ratify any agreement containing the investor-state arbitration mechanism—in the United States, for example, all treaties must be ratified by two thirds of the Senate—, critics of investor-state arbitration's democratic legitimacy argue governmental functions such as judicial proceedings simply cannot be delegated to private actors unaccountable to the democratic public. Indeed, "the direct democratic legitimation of [ISA]" premised upon the "consent of the relevant States" is, at best, "tenuous" for the following reasons.[135] First, the treaty commitments that delegate decision-making power to arbitral tribunals endure significantly beyond existence of any democratic consensus authorizing such a delegation in the first place, and are often extremely difficult to modify.[136] Treaties are thus "exceptions to ordinary lawmaking" because "they impose obligations on a country that a nation's legislature cannot thereafter amend or undo" and thus violate the basic rule of "democratic legislation [] that law made today is always subject to repeal through the ordinary democratic process tomorrow."[137] Treaties, in other words, lay claim to constitutional authority

---

132 Brower & Blanchard, *supra* note 53 at 748 (explaining that arbitrators determine only if "a state breached an obligation it undertook—in an exercise of its sovereign capacity—by concluding a treaty").

133 *See, e.g.*, Christopher Greenwood, Keynote Speech (Nov. 30, 2018), available at: http://arbitrationblog.kluwerarbitration.com/2018/11/30/does-investor-state-arbitration-have-a-future-keynote-speech-by-sir-christopher-greenwood/.

134 Brower & Schill, *supra* note 89 at 490.

135 Kingsbury & Schill, *supra* note 11 at 42.

136 *Id.*

137 Jed Rubenfeld, *Unilateralism and Constitutionalism*, 78 N.Y.U. L. Rev. 1971, 2007 (2004).

through force that a democratic legislature cannot revoke without requiring the process of "democratic mobilization and participation" through which states enact constitutions.[138]

Second, institutions more directly implicated in democratic processes possess little oversight over arbitral tribunals considering the limited input states wield in the constitution of the tribunal (appointing no more than one of three arbitrators), and the lack of meaningful review exerted by state courts or legislative bodies following the tribunal's issuance of an award.[139] Accordingly, delegation of authority to ISA tribunals leaves democratically-legitimate bodies without any means for overseeing or supervising that delegation of authority, even if the initial delegation constitutes a legitimate action.

Third, just as a state would struggle to legitimate an attempt to delegate the interpretation of its laws or constitutions to private actors, so too does a state struggle to legitimate the delegation of authority to ISA tribunals. Certain functions of public law simply cannot retain legitimacy upon delegation to private actors because those private actors owe no obligations to the polity of the state whose actions they review. Accordingly, proponents of the democratic legitimacy of ISA may not rest their defense entirely on the fact that states enter into investment agreements through politically-legitimate processes; although this argument provides a powerful (if not necessarily dispositive) defense of the state's initial accession to an investment agreement, it does not justify the continued delegation of governmental authority to ISA tribunals indefinitely into the future.

Another defense of ISA against the democratic legitimacy challenge argues that the institution cannot constitute an illegitimate constraint on a state's ability to regulate because respondent states generally prevail in investor-initiated disputes in which an arbitral tribunal issues an award. The relevance of this fact alone remains dubious even absent closer examination because the mere fact that states generally prevail does not necessarily render legitimate the process by which non-state actors preside over state regulatory decisions. And the statistics' importance to the arguments advanced by defenders of ISA is difficult to overstate.[140]

But mere recitation of respondent states' success rates in ISA does not establish that the institution favors states or investors. The selection effect, or

---

138 *Id.*

139 Kingsbury & Schill, *supra* note 11 at 42.

140 *See* Brower & Ahmad, *supra* note 65 at 1157 (emphasizing that respondent states prevail in most investor-initiated disputes).

Priest-Klein hypothesis,[141] has long established that "the observation of hotly contested trials is therefore wholly consistent with the underlying rules that are skewed toward the plaintiff, toward the defendant, or toward neither side" because "the total mass of cases brought will, by the time of trial, be reduced" in the direction of the underlying bias because either the plaintiffs or "defendants will be able to settle many cases on favorable terms", depending upon the direction of bias.[142] In other words, even if the substantive standards of investor-state arbitration heavily favored investors, investors would still not prevail on more than fifty percent of the claims adjudicated by an arbitral tribunal because, assuming symmetrical access to information concerning the strength of each claims, parties would settle both the very weak and very strong claims prior to arbitration. Of course, the political and economic context of ISA ensures that even if both parties possessed perfect information, the predicted success rate of fifty percent would not necessarily hold. States, for example, may wish to signal to domestic constituencies unwillingness to bow to foreign investors and settle cases, thereby bringing even those cases in which the investors have strong claims (encouraging settlement before arbitration at close to the amount claimed) or weak claims (encouraging settlement before arbitration at minimal amounts) through arbitration proceedings. Conversely, states may wish to avoid the costly reputational costs with both domestic and international constituencies of losing a public arbitration, and therefore wish to settle even "close" cases before trial.

But even if the specific formulation of the Priest-Klein hypothesis (that success rates will trend towards fifty percent as the number of cases proceeding through arbitration or trial falls) remains only true in general, it nonetheless demonstrates that ISA cannot be characterized as state-friendly merely because states prevail in the majority of cases that proceed through arbitration. Because, whatever the reasons, it is undeniable that very few disagreements or "differences" between investors and host states culminate in ISA proceedings before a tribunal, proponents of ISA cannot assume that the disputes proceeding through arbitration are representative of all investor-state disputes, and thus cannot assume that either the substance or procedure of ISA favors states due to states' success rates.[143] Despite its prominence in litigation analysis,

---

141 George L. Priest & Benjamin Klein, *The Selection of Disputes for Litigation*, 13 J. Legal Stud. 1 (1984).

142 Theodore Eisenberg, *Testing the Selection Effect: A New Theoretical Framework with Empirical Tests*, 19 J. Legal Stud. 339 (1990).

143 *See* W. Michael Reisman, *International Investment Arbitration and ADR: Married but Best Living Apart*, 24 ICSID Rev. 185 (2009) (explaining that there is in fact "very little" "third-party dispute resolution in the field of international investment" because most disputes

investor-state arbitration has yet to engage the selection effect,[144] and its proponents blindly maintain that the institution cannot favor investors because respondent states prevail in most investor-initiated disputes.[145]

A forth response, and perhaps most difficult for the legitimacy challenge to refute, argues that the use of private tribunals to enforce investment obligations is no different than any other manifestation of international law, in which a state cannot be the adjudicator of its own alleged violations of its international obligations.[146] This attempt to justify the legitimacy of ISA argues that all forms of international law constrain state's sovereign action, and ISA only constraints state action in a way that the state, presumably through democratic processes, previously agreed upon.[147] In other words, just as states authorize international courts to preside over challenges to, for example, human rights violations through the ratification of treaties, so too may states authorize private arbitral tribunals to preside over investment disputes.[148]

---

or differences between foreign investors and host states do not reach the stage of a full-fledged ISA proceedings).

144 *See, e.g.*, Susan D. Franck, Lindsey E. Wylie, *Predicting Outcomes in Investment Treaty Arbitration*, 65 Duke L. J. 459, 461 (2015).

145 Brower & Ahmad, *supra* note 65 at 1159 (noting that "statistics confirm[] that States win in a majority of investment cases"); Franck, *supra* note 91 at 440; Behn, *supra* note 87.

146 Brower & Blanchard, *supra* note 53 at 721 ("The broadly stated objection that investment treaties limit state discretion or "reduce sovereignty" is actually a challenge that applies against the whole of international law. In the international investment regime, states agree to limit their discretion in the treatment of foreign investors in exchange for benefits that include increased attractiveness to foreign capital, a stable economic and legal environment, improved infrastructure and services to citizens, and more efficient and environmentally sound manufacturing and energy production. Similarly, via treaties, states have agreed to restrict their handling of environmental pollutants in exchange for a cleaner planet, to compel certain treatment of aliens within their borders in exchange for reciprocal treatment of their own citizens abroad, and to improve the treatment of their own citizens by promoting human rights and the rule of law."); Brower & Schill, *supra* note 89 at 471 (explaining that "[i]nternational courts and tribunals are, in contrast to their domestic counterparts, in the unique situation of having to defend themselves on a regular basis against attacks on their legitimacy as mechanisms for resolving disputes about the scope and limits of state sovereignty.").

147 Brower & Blanchard, *supra* note 53 at 702 ("The increasing use of "sovereignty constraining" rhetoric should concern international lawyers generally, because it is in fact a challenge to foundational principles of international law that is the handmaiden of popular suspicions of international cooperation, "globalization," and multilateralism.").

148 *Id.* at 722 ("Further, it is a fundamental rule of international law that states may not override their international obligations by contrary national law. The Permanent Court of International Justice (PCIJ) and the ICJ have affirmed repeatedly that treaty obligations should not be interpreted to permit a state party to be the judge of its own case."); Schill, *supra* note 107 at 86 ("International investment law, therefore, shares core

But international tribunals of all kind face the same legitimacy challenges, and we cannot necessarily presume certain exercises of supranational authority to be legitimate by reference to others. Indeed, the current populist and nationalist backlash has taken as its target more than just international investment arbitrations, as manifest in the populist Brexit movement in the United Kingdom which developed in part as a response to subjecting British legislation and regulatory decisions to European review and control.[149] The historical reluctance of the United States to accede to sovereignty-constraining supranational bodies presents a similar legitimacy challenge.[150] Accordingly, it is not enough to rest ISA's democratic legitimacy on the legitimacy of other bodies whose democratic credentials remain in dispute, though the connection does emphasize the broader crisis facing the international liberal order.

Moreover, even if supranational judicial review of a state's actions in, for example, the human rights context constitutes a democratically legitimated exercise of sovereign power by a supranational actor, it does not necessarily follow that the same legitimation process applies to private arbitrators presiding over investment disputes. The rights enforced by an international court presiding over a human rights challenge to state action can legitimately be understood to underpin a democratic society, and can thus be legitimated in the same manner as judicial review of legislation writ large.[151] In other words, there exists a difference in kind with regard to the legitimization of human or political rights enforced by international courts under human rights treaties, and the economic rights enforced by arbitral tribunals under investment agreements.

Professor Stephan Schill has nonetheless advanced one such attempt to analogize human rights public law with investment law.[152] This approach requires accepting that the protections afforded to foreign investors in investment agreements embody and concretize the protections afforded to all property owners under a natural law-esque amalgamation of international and domestic legal principles. Schill argues: "this comparative public law approach results

functional similarities with domestic administrative and constitutional review of government conduct at the domestic as well as the international level, including under various human rights instruments, such as the European Convention on Human Rights.").

149 Posner, *supra* note 12 at 809 (explaining Brexit as part of a broader backlash against sovereignty-eroding exercises of power, particularly when international institutions operate ineffectively).

150 *See generally* Rubenfeld, *supra* note 137.

151 *See, e.g.*, Freeman, *supra* note 121 (explaining that judicial review preserves the equal exercise of political rights).

152 *See* Schill, *supra* note 107 at 101.

in the determination of general principles recognized in the principal public law systems. These principles then can be, and absent a contrary indication in the treaty in question must be, applied as a source of international law when interpreting the standards contained in international investment treaties. At the same time, general principles of public law also have to be applied to the activity of arbitral tribunals themselves. In this context, comparative public law can lead to a better understanding of the role and the powers of investment treaty tribunals in relation to the parties to the dispute and also to clarify the limits and methods of permissible judicial law-making in international investment law."[153] But by deriving the legal principles to be applied by tribunals in investor-initiated disputes from a transnational ether, however, this approach risks negating the sole democratically legitimate inputs to the institution of ISA already existing: the investment agreement itself, which reflects not general principles of law but the specific intent of the two or more states that the negotiated and reached the agreement.

Accordingly, there remain significant obstacles to the legitimation of ISA. Although a number of defenses of the institution against the democratic-legitimacy challenge have been advanced, none conclusively guarantee the legitimacy of ISA.

Part 3: Reforming Investor-State Arbitration

This Part will address efforts to reform the institution of ISA. ISA has already undergone, and will continue to undergo, a number of incremental changes in the precise contours of the protections afforded to investors, the methods for selecting arbitrators, the transparency of the proceedings, the capacity for states to file counterclaims, and other ad hoc or even systematic refinements to the institution and its application. Because ISA is a function of state agreement in the form of treaties, states will always be able to exert some control over the institution's development and evolution.[154]

The provisions governing the investor-state arbitration mechanism in the Trans-Pacific Partnership, for example, contained a number of procedural and substantive modifications from previous treaties. Procedurally, the modified provisions in the Trans-Pacific Partnership aimed to enhance the mechanism's transparency; substantively, the modified provisions sought to enhance a host state's ability to protect its citizens, so long as a viable regulatory purpose

153 *Id.*

154 Roberts, *supra* note 56.

justified the protections in question.[155] Nonetheless, the U.S. abandoned the TPP during the administration of then-President Trump due to domestic pressure, including pressure towards the inclusion of ISA provisions, from both wings of the political spectrum.[156] The investor-state arbitration mechanism in the TPP provided one of the points most susceptible to pressure, and was only minimally defended by purported proponents of trade agreement, despite significant criticism. Accordingly, ISA's survival depends on more than the incremental modifications made during the TPP-negotiation process.

Our aim is not to minimize the efficacy or purpose of these reforms; these efforts to refine investor-state arbitration are necessary for progress and have enhanced the quality of arbitral awards and the process by which tribunals arrived at those awards since the institution's inception half a century ago. As the American experience with the TPP demonstrates, however, these comparatively minor modifications will do little to legitimate investor-state arbitration itself so long as the political backlash continues against both fundamental components of the grand bargain that produced the institution of ISA: the desirability of increasing the availability and decreasing the cost of foreign capital, and the use of private arbitrators rather than national judiciaries to resolve disputes arising from foreign investments.

Accordingly, the following sections will address the two approaches to reforming the institution of ISA. Employing, in part, Professor Anthea Roberts' grouping of the existing proposals for reform articulated by states in the UNCITRAL working group,[157] we divide the proposals for reform into two categories: incremental and systemic. By incremental reform, we refer to the relatively minor modifications to the system and the standards applied that characterize the evolution of the institution of ISA in the half-century since its inception. These incremental reforms are internal because they emerge internally and seek internal solutions to the problems facing ISA; the proponents of these reforms reside within the investor-state arbitration community of practitioners and arbitrators, and the reforms aim to resolve the issues that implicate the practitioners' and arbitrators' encounters with the institution of investor-state arbitration.

As we will explain, these internal efforts towards incremental reform constitute little more than an embrace of the status quo in ISA. First, the principles of

155 Resar, *supra* note 96.

156 *See, e.g.*, Eric Bradner, Trump's TPP Withdrawal: 5 Things to Know, CNN (Jan. 23, 2017), available at: https://www.cnn.com/2017/01/23/politics/trump-tpp-things-to-know/index.html.

157 Anthea Roberts, *Incremental Systemic and Paradigmatic Reform of Investor-State Arbitration*, 112 Am. J. Int'l L. 410, 416–17 (2018).

international law applied by arbitral tribunals exist in a state of near-constant refinement, ensuring that incremental reform in application of standards is an ongoing process. Moreover, the evolution in investment treaties ensures that the provisions establishing the protections states must afford investors develop over time, and so too do the processes by which both an investor may constitute an arbitral tribunal and that tribunal arrives at its award. In other words, incremental reform amounts to maintaining the institution of ISA and allowing its processes of self-correction to run their course. But, because these incremental refinements of ISA maintain the components of ISA subject to the aforementioned political challenges, the incremental reformists do not meaningfully engage the legitimacy and political challenges facing ISA that emerge from outside the institution, and take as their target fundamental characteristics of ISA. In other words, incremental reform will not save the institution of ISA unless the political challenges to the exportation of capital and private resolution of disputes dissipate for reasons unrelated to ISA. The first section in this Part thus addresses many of the existing proposals for incremental reform to ISA, and the inability of these incremental refinements of ISA to resolve the fundamental challenges to the institution raised in the preceding sections.

The second section then addresses the various proposals for systemic reform to the institution of ISA.[158] Systemic reform refers to attempts to modify significantly the institution of ISA without eliminating its fundamental element: the foreign investor's capacity to initiate a dispute against the state hosting the investment and be heard before a judicial body independent from the host state's own judiciary.[159] Unlike the incremental reform efforts, systemic reform acknowledges the validity of and threat posed by the emerging political challenges to the institution of ISA. Systemic reformers recognize that ISA is experiencing a crisis of political legitimacy in both traditionally capital-importing and capital-exporting states, and that the institution's survival thus requires changes designed to enhance state and popular support. To this end,

158 Roberts' taxonomy of reforms adds an additional category, paradigmatic reforms, these reforms amount to a negation of ISA, as they require shifts away from either independent resolution of disputes or the private right of action granted to investors. *Id.* at 420 (defining paradigm shifters as those "who dismiss the existing system as irrevocably flawed and in need of wholesale replacement" because paradigm shifters "reject the utility of investors' making international claims against states, whether before arbitral tribunals or international courts").

159 *Id.* (defining "systemic reforms" as those who "see merit in retaining an investors' ability to file claims directly on the international level, but view investor-state arbitration as a seriously flawed system for dealing with such claims. They champion more significant systemic reforms, such as replacing investor-state arbitration with a multilateral investment court and appellate body.").

the European Union has proposed a permanent international investment law court of first instance and appellate body designed to enhance the consistency and legitimacy of ISA awards. Because the EU's proposal for the creation of a permanent trial and appellate body dominates discussion of systemic reform to ISA, our discussion of the contours and drawbacks of that proposal compose much of the second section.

We conclude that though intended to alleviate the populist and democratic challenges to ISA, the creation of a permanent trial and appellate body would only accentuate those challenges. Specifically, the creation of a permanent supranational body to preside over challenges to a state's regulatory decisions would do nothing to enhance the democratic legitimacy of the awards rendered, and, if anything, would only heighten sovereignty concerns in those states with political traditions skeptical of supranational authorities, such as the United States and United Kingdom. Instead of alleviating concerns of non-state entities exercising judicial powers, the creation of a permanent trial and appellate body merely moves the non-state adjudicatory entity from the private level as exists in the current model of ISA to the supranational level. But both the nationalist and democratic-legitimacy challenges to private ISA apply with equal force to supranational governance, as is apparent in, for example, the unusual agreement between the far left and far right in British politics regarding the purported undemocratic and oppressive nature of the European Union.

While the creation of an appellate body attempts to imbue ISA with legitimacy by mimicking the form of national judiciaries, an alternative approach would instead more closely embed ISA within state judiciaries. Though potentially inimical to the grand bargain's promise of dispute settlement conducted before arbitrators or other adjudicators independent from either the host state of the investment of the investor's home state, national courts provide one available mechanism for the control of ISA tribunals. Because national courts must review arbitral awards when parties seek to enforce or annul the awards, national courts provide one underexplored mechanism of control for ISA. But investor-initiated disputes often challenge judicial decisions; granting the same judiciaries that an arbitral award determined breached the investment agreements substantive provisions power to more closely review that award would undermine the very purpose of ISA. And granting such review power to another state's courts—as could occur if the parties agree to seat an arbitration outside the state hosting the initial investment—would do nothing to enhance the democratic legitimacy of the award, as the judiciary of an unrelated state is obviously entirely removed from the democratic processes of the host state. The third section thus explains why the enhancement of the scrutiny with which national judiciaries review investment arbitration awards and decisions would fatally undermine ISA's foundational promise of neutral and independent adjudication for investor-initiated disputes.

Thus, we conclude the reforms that ISA could undertake either: (1) fail to fully acknowledge, much less resolve, the political challenges ISA faces in the case of incremental reform proposals; (2) acknowledge but either fail to resolve or in fact exacerbate the democracy deficit ISA faces in the case of the European Union's proposal to create a permanent investment court; or (3) fail to retain the fundamental premise of the grand bargain that underlies ISA in the case of attempts to enhance the control exerted by national judiciaries over the ISA process. Because no single reform (or even amalgamation of reforms) can thus legitimate ISA and insulate the institution from the political challenges it faces, ISA's survival depends upon the national political decisions to more equitably distribute the gains from an increase in the availability of foreign investment that ISA promises to deliver.

1 *Incremental and Internal Reform*

One approach to address the perceived challenges to the institution of ISA involves attempts to modify the application of existing standards, rather than modify the process through which private arbitrators apply standards.[160] These modifications take the form of reformulated protections a state must provide to foreign investors. These modifications grant a host state greater freedom to regulate in the public interest, or authoritatively interpret ambiguous treaty provisions that previously facilitated inconsistent arbitral awards and awards that compensated investors when the states party to the treaty did not intend for investors to be compensated.[161] Because ISA exists only pursuant to the treaties that contain provisions authorizing it, states propose to adopt these incremental reforms through new treaties or the adoption of authoritative interpretations by bodies authorized to issue binding interpretations of investment agreements.[162]

160 *See, e.g.*, Hueckel, *supra* note 81 (arguing that the legitimacy deficiency investor-state arbitration faces "can be remedied by addressing the existing structural weaknesses in the way states delegate and control the power they transfer to tribunals. Specifically, this should be done through a concerted move away from open-ended standards. Instead, negotiators should look to more specifically drafted rules and interpretative guidelines to control arbitration outcomes ex ante….").

161 Roberts, *supra* note 157 at 416 (explaining the incrementalist positions adopted by, inter alia, Chile, Russia, and the United States in the UNCITRAL working group tasked with addressing reforms to the investor-state arbitral model for investor-initiated disputes).

162 *Id.* (noting that, "[f]or example, the United States [argued] that problematic or inconsistent interpretations could be rectified by drafting new treaties in more detail or adopting authoritative interpretations" in the UNCITRAL working group).

The states party to NAFTA, for example, have employed the NAFTA Free Trade Commission to authoritatively define the scope and extent of a state's obligations under a particular protection for investors.[163] They issued an interpretation of a fair and equitable treatment while a number of ISAs concerning those provisions were pending.[164] Similar commissions exist in other investment agreements between NAFTA parties and third state, including Canada's agreements with the European Free Trade Association, Colombia, Peru, Chile, Costa Rica, Jordan and Israel; the United States' agreements including CAFTA, the U.S-Australia Free Trade Agreement, the U.S.-Chile Free Trade Agreement, and agreements with Colombia, Korea, Morocco, Oman, Panama, Peru, Rwanda, Singapore, and Uruguay; and Mexico's agreements with Japan, the European Free Trade Association, the European Union, and Israel.[165]

These incremental modifications to the institution of ISA, however, amount to a perpetuation of the status quo,[166] and thus fail to address the political challenges to ISA that dispute the institution's purpose and existence. As we explained previously, ISA is an inherently self-correcting system, both because ISA is a function of interstate contract (treaties) and because arbitrators sensitive to political concerns conduct ISA. Specifically, arbitrators are responsive to the concerns of the states whose investment agreements the arbitrators interpret, ensuring self-correction of problematic or inconsistent interpretations of investment agreements. Indeed, following concerns expressed by numerous states about foreign investment protections improperly infringing upon the state's right to regulate, arbitrators have interpreted investment agreements to ensure that states retain such authority.[167] Simultaneously,

---

163 *See, e.g.*, Stefan Matiation, *Arbitration With Two Twists: Loewen v. United States and Free Trade Commission Intervention in NAFTA Chapter 11 Disputes*, 24 U. Pa. J. Int'l Econ. L. 452, 453 (2003) (explaining how the NAFTA Free Trade Commission, composed of the trade ministers for each of the NAFTA Parties, issued an interpretation of NAFTA provisions part way through the proceedings in *Loewen v. United States*, perhaps intending to "undercut one foundation for Loewen's argument").

164 *Id.*

165 *See* Gabrielle Kaufmann-Kohler, Interpretive Powers of the Free Trade Commission and the Rule of Law, in Fifteen Years of NAFTA Chapter 11 Arbitration (2011).

166 Roberts, *supra* note 157 at 415 ("Incrementalists typically claim that any outstanding problems can be addressed adequately through targeted reforms. For example, the United States noted that problematic or inconsistent interpretations could be rectified by drafting new treaties in more detail or adopting authoritative interpretations.").

167 Brower & Schill, *supra* note 89 at 485 ("Thus, the Tribunal in *Tecnicas Medioambientales Tecmed SA v Mexico* held that '[t]he principle that the State's exercise of its sovereign powers within the framework of its police power may cause economic damage to those subject to its powers as administrator without entitling them to any compensation whatsoever is undisputable.'") (citing Tecnicas Medioambientales Teemed SA v The United Mexican States, ICSID Case No ARB(AF)/00/2, Award of (May 29, 2003) 119, available

because the existence of ISA and the obligations enforced therein depends upon state agreement, states are able to reformulate the substantive protections contained in investment agreements enforced through ISA. The ongoing multilateralization of investment protections, which occurs through multilateral investment agreements and most-favored nation clauses,[168] ensures this process continues.

ISA's evolution through both developments in arbitral case law and treaty drafting with regards to the transparency of proceedings and participation of non-investors provides a compelling example of this process. ISA in its earliest formulations faced significant criticism regarding the institution's lack of transparency, especially in comparison to national courts.[169] Indeed, proponents of reform, whether incremental or systemic, continue to voice that criticism, arguing ISA is necessarily less transparent than judicial proceedings because third parties lack the ability to participate.[170] But ISA "ceased to be hidden from public view long ago," in large part because of these criticisms.[171] Most awards are public and easily found on the internet, along with recordings or video of hearings and entire party submissions.[172] Even where parties do not agree to publish submissions or decisions, ICSID publishes excerpts of the legal reasoning of all awards, so that states and investors can understand the substantive contents of the investment protections.[173] And in July 2013, UNCITRAL adopted Transparency Rules for ISA, even amending the UNCITRAL

---

online at <http://icsid.worldbank.org/ICSID/FrontServlet?requestType=CasesRH&actionVal=showDoc&docId=DC602_En&caseld=C1 86>).

168 *See* Schill, *supra* note 103 at 561.

169 William Glaberson, NAFTA Invoked to Challenge Court Award, N.Y. TIMES, Jan. 28, 1999, at C6, available at http://www.nytimes.com/1999/01/28/business/nafta-invoked-to-challenge-court-award.html?pagewanted=print ("This is wrong and harmful to America because it substitutes for our judicial system a confidential arbitration panel that's not open to public scrutiny.").

170 EUROPEAN PARLIAMENTARY RESEARCH SERVICE BRIEFING, INVESTOR-STATE DISPUTE SETTLEMENT: STATE OF PLAY AND PROSPECTS FOR REFORM (2014).

171 Brower & Blanchard, *supra* note 53 at 716.

172 *Id.* (citing Investment Treaty Arbitration, ITA LAW, http://www.italaw.com/ (last visited Mar. 14, 2014); ICSID Cases, ICSID, https://icsid.worldbank.org/ICSID/FrontServlet?requestType=CasesRH&actionVal=ShowHome&pageName=Cases_Home (last visited Mar.14, 2014); Cases, PERMANENT CT. OF ARB., http://www.pca-cpa.org/showpage.asp?pag_id=1029 (last visited Mar. 14, 2014); Investor-State Dispute Settlement Cases, ENERGY CHARTER, http://www.encharter.org/index.php?id=213 (last visited Mar. 14, 2014).).

173 *Id.*

Arbitration Rules to require the publication of submissions and awards and hearings.[174]

The move towards third-party involvement in arbitral proceedings is similar. The UNCITRAL Transparency Rules, for example, require that tribunals constituted under the UNCITRAL Arbitration Rules permit third parties to make submissions.[175] The proposed Trans-Pacific Partnership contained similar provisions, establishing standards and procedures for amicus submissions from non-parties.[176] Even the ability of states to pursue counterclaims before an ISA tribunal has emerged, first in a dissent from a denial of an state's ability to pursue a counterclaim,[177] then as a recognized but implicit feature of investment agreements,[178] and finally as a codified fixture of proposed investment agreements.[179] Whether ISA need, or even should, accommodate the claims brought by states or third parties, however, remains an open question; despite significant criticism of the "un-reciprocal" nature of ISA,[180] third party civil groups harmed by a foreign investor's violations of a trade agreement's

174 See Press Release, United Nations Information Service, UNCITRAL Adopts Transparency Rules for Treaty-Based Investor-State Arbitration and Amends the UNCITRAL Arbitration Rules (Dec. 18, 2013), available at http://www.unis.unvienna.org/unis/pressrels/2013/unisl186.html; UNCITRAL Rules on Transparency in Treaty-based Investor-State Arbitration, UNCTIRAL (Jan. 2014), available at http://www.uncitral.org/pdf/english/texts/arbitration/rules-on-transparency/pre-release-UNCITRAL-Rules-on-Transparency.pdf.

175 *Id.*

176 *See* Ko-Yung Tung, *Investor-State Dispute Settlement under the Trans-Pacific Partnership*, 23 Cal. Int'l L. J. 19, 22 (2015) (noting that, "in recognition that many investor-state arbitration proceedings involve public issues and other stakeholders, recent investment treaties, such as ICSID and the 2012 U.S. Model BIT, explicitly permit a tribunal, in its discretion, to accept amicus submissions.").

177 Roussalis v. Romania, ICSID ARB/06/01, Award, ¶¶ 868, 872 (Dec. 7, 2011), available at http://www.italaw.com/sites/default/files/case-documents/ita0723.pdf.

178 *See* Antoine Goetz & Consorts et S.A. Affinage des Metaux v. Republique du Burundi, ICSID Case No. ARB/01/2, Sentence, ¶¶ 278–79 (June 21, 2012), *available at* http://www.italaw.com/sites/default/files/case-documents/italaw1086.pdf; Inmaris Perestroika Sailing Maritime Services GmbH v. Ukraine, ICSID Case No. ARB/08/8, Award, ¶¶ 431–32 (Mar. 1, 2012), *available at* https://icsid.worldbank.org/ICSID/FrontServlet?requestType=CasesRH&actionVal=showDoc&docId=DC3296_En&caseId=C320.

179 The Trans-Pacific Partnership Agreement, for example, expressly authorized counterclaims "in connection with the factual and legal basis of the claim." *See, generally*, Resar, *supra* note 96 at 184.

180 Timothy Meyer and Ganesh Sitaraman, A Blueprint for a New American Trade Policy, Dec. 2018 (arguing that a future standing ISA court should possess jurisdiction to hear claims brought by injured civil society groups for violations of the labor and environment chapters of trade agreements).

environmental or labor provisions, for example, have recourse through the judicial systems of the country hosting the investment.

Thus, the "criticism that investment treaties afford unilateral benefits to investors presents a limited and in fact contorted picture of investor-state relations" by "disregard[ing] the fact that the host state," and other third parties "already possess a power that the foreign investor lacks."[181] The remedies available to host states, even those unable to pursue counterclaims, are extensive, as they may impose sanctions on the investor for violations of the host state's own law and enforce those sanctions against the assets of the investment project.[182] In short, the "un-reciprocal" nature of investor-initiated disputes adopted by ISA is necessary to balance the asymmetrical relationship that would otherwise exist when an foreign investor challenges a host state's actions in that host state's own courts. And reciprocity before the investment tribunal provides little additional value to the state because the state already has numerous avenues for penalizing an investor's violation of its legal obligations.[183] Regardless of the merits of the underlying change, though, the evolutionary capability of ISA is readily apparent: in under a decade, counterclaims by states in ISA proceedings became available and codified in future agreements.

Investment agreements may also create independent bodies tasked with issuing authoritative interpretations of the agreements' substantive provisions, thereby guiding arbitral tribunals towards the states' agreed-upon understanding.[184] While not necessarily authoritative, non-state actors such as international bar associations and UNCITRAL working groups may also play a similar role in shaping tribunals' understanding of substantive provisions.[185]

Indeed, the views of its proponents demonstrate that incremental reform amounts to the status quo in ISA. Reports indicate that the Russian Federation, for example, has strongly urged the UNCITRAL working group to refrain from systemic changes to the institution of ISA by arguing that inconsistencies in interpretation of investment agreement provisions reflect an optimized approach to investor-state disputes. Because ISA in its current form necessarily

181 Brower & Schill, *supra* note 89 at 482.

182 *Id.*

183 Brower & Blanchard, *supra* note 53 at 712 ("Investors are bound by the law of the host state and by their contractual obligations. As sovereigns, host states have many tools at their disposal for responding to investor breaches, including civil and criminal penalties, legal actions for breach of contract in their own courts, and political pressure. The very nature of the relationship means that the foreign investor will typically have assets in the host state, guaranteeing enforcement leverage.").

184 *See, e.g.*, Matiation, *supra* note 163 at 453.

185 *See, e.g.*, International Bar Association Report, Consistency Efficiency and Transparency in Investment Treaty Arbitration (Nov. 2018).

provides ad hoc resolutions to investor-initiated disputes, ISA capacity for parties to reach unique agreements that reflect individualized situations is an advantage of the existing decentralized arbitral order.[186]

Accordingly, arguments in support of incremental reforms in response to the political challenges ISA faces suggest that ISA need only continue on its current trajectory.[187] Because the incremental reform model recognizes only internal challenges to ISA such as tribunals arriving at inconsistent or incorrect interpretations of substantive investment protections, incremental reformers efforts engage only peripherally with ISA's broader legitimacy crisis.

To note that incremental reform does little to enhance the legitimacy of third party arbitration of investor-initiated disputes against states, or to encourage the free flow of international investment, does not refute the utility or importance of these reforms. These incremental reforms serve to enhance the quality of the arbitral awards produced, and over time will enhance the institutions bureaucratic rational-legal legitimacy.[188] To the extent that ISA legitimates its investor-initiated review of state actions through the rationality and legality of its outcomes, the legitimacy of ISA, "in Weberian terms … depends, at least in part, on the legality and rationality of its design, its processes, and the technical quality and persuasiveness of the reasons tribunals give in explaining and justifying their decisions."[189] The incremental reforms that emerge out of ISA's self-correcting evolution help guarantee and enhance the legality and rationality of the institutions' design, processes, and outputs (awards and decisions). Accordingly, the continuation of incremental reform is vital the institution's viability in the long-term.

Incremental reforms are thus vital to the extent that ISA's future legitimacy hinges upon its instrumental capabilities, meaning the institution's capacity to deliver upon its promises to the relevant parties (capital-importing states, capital-exporting states, and investors).[190] To this end, ISA's viability will depend upon its ability to deliver "effective justice in the form of readily available, competent, neutral, and procedurally informal (compared to the

186 Roberts, *supra* note 157 at 415 (explaining that the Russian Federation has argued before the UNCITRAL working group that "concerns about inconsistent decisions are a natural and positive consequence of the bilateral nature of investment treaties" because "the ability of parties to strike particular deals is 'an advantage of the system and not a disadvantage'").

187 *Id.* at 415 ("Incrementalists tend to downplay the severity of the existing system's problems by suggesting, for instance, that the concerns raised are merely matters of perception rather than reality.").

188 Kingsbury & Schill, *supra* note 11 at 41.

189 *Id.*

190 Puig, *supra* note 22.

formalities imposed by public international law) processes for resolving disputes involving investment abroad."[191] ISA's legitimacy need not only depend upon its capacity to enhance foreign investment, then, as the institution serves other significant purposes including the de-escalation through private resolution of international economic conflicts.[192] From a purely instrumental perspective, then, enhancing ISA's capacity to provide a depoliticized international economic conflicts thus enhances ISA's legitimacy.[193]

But such incremental reform decidedly fails to address the externally-initiated legitimacy crises ISA currently faces, because these incremental reforms retain the fundamental characteristics of ISA that are the object of political challenges: the promotion of foreign investment, and the resolution before private actors of the disputes that arise therefrom.[194] Indeed, as we will argue in the final section, the *inter*national legal task of optimizing the existing institution of ISA to ensure internal support remains an important process; it is merely a process insufficient to ensure ISA's survival absent the *intra*national political tasks of ensuring political support for foreign investment by more equitably distributing the products of that investment.

2 *Systemic Reform through Permanent Courts and Appellate Bodies*

This section addresses the potential for systemic reform that preserves the fundamental compromise embodied in the institution of ISA (investor-initiated actions before independent adjudicators to enforce a host state's obligations under an investment agreement) while modifying the process by which that

---

191 *Id.* at 481, 483 (With ISA "and the threat of neutrally-administered international dispute settlement technique—the argument follows—even the most sturdy state can become attractive for investors, including states who had not originally stipulated international forms of dispute settlement in individual contracts.").

192 *Id.* at 487 ("In short, this second source of legitimacy originates from the attempts to compartmentalize international economic conflicts and the consequent insulation of inter-state politics through a formal legal processes.").

193 *Id.* at 484–85 (ISA "attempts to create a mutually beneficial setting for all the parties involved. It does so by compartmentalizing potentially daunting conflicts between states into individual disputes between investors and states. This-some argue-helps to "de-politicize" internationally distressing conflicts, liberating a tense space between states to be employed for building constructive relationships. This approach tames the role of power in world politics, favoring long-term cooperation and diplomatic solidarity.").

194 Schill, *supra* note 107 at 70 (explaining that a "system-internal approach" characteristic of the incrementalist reform position "above all, would leave untouched the trust investors have development vis-à-vis international arbitration as an independent and impartial dispute resolution mechanism, while making necessary concessions towards demands coming from outside international investment law in terms of transparency, openness, predictability, and respect for noninvestment concerns.").

promise is realized. Unlike incremental reform, which denies either the existence or validity of political legitimacy challenges ISA faces, systemic reform acknowledges that ISA's durability depends upon modifications to the institution of ISA intended to enhance the institution's legitimacy.

At least in part, these systemic reforms seek to respond to the perceived legitimacy deficiencies of investor-state arbitration. Indeed, the influence of the legitimacy challenge to ISA is apparent in the proposed modifications to institution of ISA developed following the 2009 Treaty of Lisbon, delegating to the European Commission authority for the negotiation of investment-agreements binding upon all members of the European Union.[195]

Specifically, in response to the perceived lack of democratic legitimacy, the EU has sought render investor-state arbitration more judicial by mimicking the form of presumably legitimate judicial bodies.[196] The European Commission would, following the trend towards supranational governance embodied by the European Union itself,[197] create a permanent and supranational court to adjudicate investor-state disputes.[198] And with its decision in *Achmea* and subsequent Opinion 1/17,[199] the European Court of Justice has pushed ISA in this direction. Specifically, while *Achmea* held ISA provisions in intra-EU investment agreements were incompatible with the law of the European Union because such tribunals are insufficiently grounded within the national judiciaries approved by the European Court of Justice, Opinion 1/17

195 Simon Lester, *The ISDS Controversy: How We Got Here and Where Next*, CATO Institute: Commentary (July 1, 2016), available at: https://www.cato.org/publications/commentary/isds-controversy-how-we-got-here-where-next.

196 Puig & Shaffer, *supra* note 39 at 367 ("Prominently, the European Union (EU) has promoted a multilateral investment court system where private investors retain standing to file claims directly against states. At its core, this "systemic" change would create a tribunal of first instance and an appellate body, with the judges having fixed terms, paid a regular salary, and selected on a random basis from a roster designated by states. These judges accordingly would be restricted from acting as counsel in other cases.").

197 *See, e.g.*, Posner, *supra* note 12 at 801 (explaining how the "the institutional structures set up within [the European Union] … were supervised and enforced by the European Court of Justice (ECJ). The result was a transformation of Westphalian international law into a type of quasiconstitutional law. With the newly dominant role of the ECJ, rule-of-law values would, at least at the margin, displace power politics.").

198 European Commission, Investment in TTIP and Beyond—The Path for Reform, Enhancing the Right to Regulate and Moving from Current ad hoc Arbitration Towards an Investment Court, at 11 (May 2015), available at http://trade.ec.europa.eu/doclib/docs/2015/may/tradoc_153408.PDF ("the EU should pursue the creation of one permanent court").

199 *See* Opinion 1/17 of the Court of Justice of the European Union, (Apr. 30, 2019), *available at*: http://curia.europa.eu/juris/document/document.jsf?text=&docid=213502&pageIndex=0&doclang=EN&mode=lst&dir=&occ=first&part=1&cid=4976548.

expressly authorized ISA under a particular set of circumstances. Specifically, adjudicating the legality of the the ISA provision under the Comprehensive Economic and Trade Agreement between the EU and Canada ("CETA") under European Union law, Opinion 1/17 held that ISA provisions are enforceable where a tribunal is constituted under an investment agreement that limits an arbitration panel to interpreting the investment agreement itself, rather than European Union law, and provides for the procedural protections available in national judiciaries. The effect of this ruling will be to push ISA towards a more permanent, institutionalized supranational governance body resembling the European Union itself: a permanent multilateral investment court, discussed *supra*.

Proposals for creation of a permanent court for the adjudication of investment disputes emerged in the early twenty-first century, when inconsistency in ad hoc tribunal's application of substantive investment provisions generated calls for a permanent appellate body.[200] As the democratic legitimacy challenge to ISA gained force amongst both publics and elected officials, the proposal for an appellate body transformed into a proposal for a standing court that would both adjudicate disputes in the first instance and hear appeals arising from the lower trial court's decisions. By transferring the power to adjudicate investment disputes from private tribunals to a permanent court constituted with state input, this proposal for systemic reform seeks to legitimate the institution of investor-state arbitration by mimicking the *form* of presumably legitimate judicial bodies: national and supranational courts.[201]

To this end, the European Commission has proposed a modified version of ICSID for use in the Transatlantic Trade and Investment Partnership ("TTIP"),[202] establishing a permanent "Tribunal of First Instance" and appellate

200 *See, e.g.*, Brower II, *supra* note 45 at 93–94 ("[C]ontinuation of ad hoc arbitration, followed by review by a standing appellate tribunal, and supervised by an accountable, transparent, and publicly accessible Free Trade Commission, seems best suited to promote a legitimate investment regime."); Johanna Kalb, *Creating an ICSID Appellate Body*, 10 UCLA J. INT'L L. & FOR. AFF. 179. 202 (2005).

201 *See* Roberts, *supra* note 157 at 416 (explaining that the "European Union argued [] investment claims are based on public international law treaties and involve public law disputes in which generally worded constitutional-like clauses are applied to regulate the sovereign actions of states vis-à-vis investors. In similar areas of law, states have favored the establishment of permanent bodies with full-time, tenured adjudicators, such as the WTO Appellate Body and the European Court of Human Rights.").

202 Office of the United States Trade Representative, available at: https://ustr.gov/ttip (describing the "Transatlantic Trade and Investment Partnership (T-TIP) is an ambitious, comprehensive, and high-standard trade and investment agreement being negotiated between the United States and the European Union (EU)").

body.[203] The Tribunal of First Instance would consist of fifteen judges, one-third nationals of EU member states, one-third nationals of the United States, and one-third nationals of third countries; under the EC-proposed terms, every three judge panel would reflect this breakdown of nationalities.[204] The judges would serve six-year terms, renewable once.[205] Similarly, the "Appeal Tribunal" would be composed of six "Members", again reflecting the one-third EU-member state nationals, one-third US nationals, and one-third country nationals breakdown, and who must "have demonstrated expertise in public international law."[206] The arbitrators composing both the appeal tribunals and courts of first instance would be paid a regular monthly salary (even when not presiding over investment disputes), serve for fixed and tenured terms, and agree to a set of conflict and ethical obligations to ensure independence from the "revolving door" between advocate and arbitrator that is so prevalent in ISA's current form.[207] Both states and investors could appeal the court of first instance's decisions for errors of law, manifest errors of fact, and the grounds provided in Article 52 of the ICSID Convention.[208] Moreover, the appeal tribunal could either modify, reverse, or remand for further consideration the court of first instance's decision.[209]

Whether a permanent and supranational body would successfully accomplish the aims pursued by states and investors in the Grand Bargain that produced ISA remains in dispute. Critics of a permanent investment court challenge the proposal on two distinct theoretical grounds,[210] even apart from concerns that an appellate body would undermine the finality of arbitral

203 *Id.* at 18, 19.

204 *Id.*

205 *Id.*

206 Joint Interpretative Instrument on the Comprehensive Economic and Trade Agreement (CETA) Between Canada and the European Union and its Member States, OJ L 11, 14 (Jan. 2017) [hereinafter CETA]; European Commission Press Release, The EU and Vietnam Finalize Landmark Trade Deal (Dec. 2, 2015), at Art. 8.27(4) http://trade.ec.europa.eu/doclib/press/index.cfm?id=1409.

207 This would be true only after states had fully constituted the permanent investment court. In the transitional period, "the Tribunal members would be paid a monthly retainer complemented by the scheduled ICSID hourly fees when they serve on a Tribunal, and they would not be barred from working on arbitration cases." Puig & Shaffer, *supra* note 39 at n.216.

208 *Id.*

209 *Id.*

210 There also exist practical objections to the creation of a permanent investment court. *See, e.g.*, Roberts, *supra* note 157 at 420 (explaining that "a prominent arbitrator, Judge Stephen M. Schwebel, explained that his 'fundamental objection' to the European Union's proposal is that it would replace a system that 'on any objective analysis works reasonably

awards.[211] First, some proponents of the existing ad hoc system for resolving disputes argue that a permanent international investment court would fail to promote international peace by depoliticizing investment disputes.[212] Commentators note that "[e]ven elections to the International Court of Justice ("ICJ") are politicized," ensuring that "there is no way of depoliticizing the appointment process of the proposed investment court."[213] We do not find this objection compelling. A politicized appointment process for an supranational court is not the same as a politicized international economic dispute, and the consequences of disagreement regarding the appointment of a particular arbitrator to an adjudicatory body (as the appointment would not be made for a particular dispute) pale in comparison to the consequences of disagreement directly over a state's protection of a foreign national's investment. The former can only heighten diplomatic tension between states, while the latter entails diplomatic protection and the possibility of interstate conflict.[214]

Even if the process by which arbitrators were appointed by states to the permanent investment court were highly politicized, it does not follow that states would politicize the disputes over which that court would preside, nor would it render such a permanent court dependent and partial to states.[215] In the international context, appointment to the Dispute Settlement Body (DSB) of the World Trade Organization may be highly politicized, but compliance with decisions issued by the body remains high.[216] In the national context, too, judicial appointments may be highly contentious and partisan without necessarily politicizing the disputes over which those judicial appointees preside. Even if interjecting politics into certain pre-dispute processes, the creation of a permanent investment court is thus unlikely to return the international

---

well" with "a system that would face substantial problems of coherence, rationalization, negotiation, ratification, establishment, functioning and financing'").

211 For concerns regarding finality, *see, e.g.*, Ian Laird & Rebecca Askew, *Finality Versus Consistency: Does Investor-State Arbitration Need an Appellate System*; 7 J. App. Practice Proc. 285 (2005).

212 Puig & Shaffer, *supra* note 39 at 400 (explaining that a permanent arbitral body may not fully depoliticize disputes).

213 Charles N. Brower & Jawad Ahmad, *From the Two-Headed Nightingale to the Fifteen-Headed Hydra: The Many Follies of the Proposed International Investment Court*, 41 Ford. Int'l L. J. 791, 793 (2018).

214 *Supra* Part 1.

215 Brower & Blanchard, *supra* note 53 at 766 ("States delegate lawmaking authority to international courts and tribunals as trustees to make their treaty commitments credible. Thus the key feature of international tribunals is that they be independent and impartial").

216 *See, e.g.*, H.E. Shahid Bashir, "WTO Dispute Settlement Body Developments in 2012," available at: https://www.wto.org/english/tratop_e/dispu_e/bashir_13_e.htm (estimating the compliance rate with DSB recommendations and rulings to be about 90 percent).

community to the highly politicized resolution of investment disputes that prevailed under the system of diplomatic protection, often involving the use or threatened use of force.

The second and more compelling objection to the creation of a permanent appellate body argues a supranational body fails to remedy (or even accentuates) the democratic legitimacy problem posed by non-state actors presiding over a state's regulatory decisions. Although a permanent investment court would allow for (indirect) democratic participation in the constitution of the adjudicatory body presiding over investor-initiated disputes, both in terms of the procedural and substantive contours under which the judicial body operates and the individual arbitrators states appoint to the body, the creation of a permanent, judicial body will not enhance opportunities for democratic participation in the arbitral process once constituted.[217] And the governmental input enhanced by the creation of a permanent arbitral body (a purported greater say in the constitution of the tribunal) is of dubious relevance to the disputes challenging a state's own regulatory decision. A state would not be guaranteed that the arbitrator that state appoints will play a role in the adjudication of those disputes and, indeed, would be excluded from adjudicating disputes against the state responsible for their appointment under some proposals. With regards to state input on any particular tribunal, then, the proposed permanent court may reduce democratic input below even the levels attained by existing ad hoc arbitration, in which the state can guarantee the appointment of one arbitrator on the three-arbitrator panel.

Apart from the appointment question, the creation of a permanent investment court does little to enhance the theoretical democratic legitimacy of ISA. Merely mimicking the form of national judiciaries would not imbue investment agreements with the legitimacy of national judicial review because national courts attained legitimacy not merely through their form, but through a prolonged history in which legitimation and democratic acceptance was hard-won. The diversity in structures of courts of constitutional review across democratic governments repudiates any suggestion that the mere formal structure of a judicial body is sufficient to produce democratic legitimacy: some constitutional courts review only legislation, some discrete cases or controversies; some constitutional courts are composed of members for life, some are composed of individuals serving strict term limits, and so on. A permanent body of non-governmental actors (as the European Commission proposal

217 Brower II, *supra* note 45 at 92 ("With respect to legitimacy, the fact remains that an appellate tribunal has a judicial, as opposed to a political, character and [] necessarily provides limited opportunities for democratic participation.").

requires that the members of both the Tribunal of First Instance and Appeal Tribunal not be members of any parties' national governments) does little to remedy the democratic deficiency inherent in the delegation of judicial power over a nation's regulatory decisions to supranational authorities.

The creation of a permanent investment court would effectively create a supranational judiciary to preside over questions of public and administrative law. The transfer of sovereign regulatory power (or judicial power over the exercise of that regulatory power) from national governments to such a supranational body, removed from the democratic processes in which national judiciaries are embedded, would arguably only enhance the democratic deficiencies of ISA.[218] Expectations that states generally removed from and opposed to supranational governance would accede to a permanent investment court as a remedy to the democratic deficiencies of ISA in its existing ad hoc form appear implausible.

Indeed, even members of the European Community, the body of states most familiar with and amenable to supranational governance bodies,[219] have questioned whether the creation of a permanent investment court would violate other commitments to provide access to courts, rather than specialized arbitral bodies.[220] The increasing distrust of supranational governance voiced by continental populists and the Leave Movement in the United Kingdom, notably present on both the left and right, has threatened the European Union's continued existence in its current form.[221] Other states, such as Japan, view "the proposed permanent court as 'a world legislator being in a position to decide highly sensitive and important issues without any accountability.'"[222] In other words, even if the arbitrators appointed to the permanent court derive

---

218 *See* Rubenfeld, *supra* note 137 at 2011 ("Judges may, in one sense, be nonpolitical actors, but the judiciary is nevertheless a governmental institution, embedded within a larger political process, and it makes a great difference, democratically speaking, whether adjudication occurs in national or international courts. As noted earlier, the many indirect connections between a nation's judiciary and its democratic processes are critical to ensuring that law retains its claim to legitimate authority in a society that claims to be self-governing.").

219 *See, e.g.*, Wojciech Sadurski, *Democratic Legitimacy of the European Union: A Diagnosis and Some Modest Proposals*, 32 Pol. Ybk of Int'l L. (2013) (explaining the European Union's supranational character, present in the governance the EU exerts on over state's decisions, requires enhanced democratic legitimization).

220 *See* Opinion 1/17 of the Court of Justice of the European Union, (Apr. 30, 2019), *available at*: http://curia.europa.eu/juris/document/document.jsf?text=&docid=213502&pageIndex=0&doclang=EN&mode=lst&dir=&occ=first&part=1&cid=4976548.

221 *See generally* Posner, *supra* note 12 at 813.

222 Brower & Ahmad, *supra* note 65 at 1155.

their initial authority from their appointment by states, they remain unaccountable after appointment, and therefore do not possess the democratic legitimacy necessary to overcome such challenges to ISA.

At least in the short- to medium-term, then, merely mimicking the form of judicial bodies will be insufficient to confer the democratic legitimacy of those judicial bodies onto the institution of investor-state arbitration. Though it is plausible that the institution of investor-state arbitration could attain legitimacy over the long term having adopted the form of judicial bodies, it is equally plausible that such legitimacy could be attained by the institution of investor-state arbitration in its current form. Because the mechanism by which legitimacy would be attained over time—continuity and gradual acceptance—is in no way contingent upon the form of the institution, such formal changes will not redress existing criticisms of investor-state arbitration as lacking democratic legitimacy. This is not to deny that the formal structures through which states delegate the administration of justice may implicate the democratic legitimacy of the justice administered, but rather to acknowledge that the existing proposals to restructure the administration of investor-state arbitrations do little to enhance the democratic legitimacy of the institution.

3 *State-Centric Systems of Control*

An alternative systemic (or even paradigmatic[223]) reform to the institution of investor-state arbitration would not seek to mimic national judiciaries, but rather more closely embed investor-state arbitration within national judicial bodies. Though this reform approach could take the incremental form by enhancing exhaustion requirements that mandate investors seek relief before local judiciaries prior to initiating a suit before an arbitral tribunal,[224] it is also possible to envision the reform of investment arbitration's judicial control systems, enhancing judicial review of arbitral awards. Such an approach need not be taken to the extreme of returning full authority to judicial bodies, as some states have proposed as an alternative to ISA.[225] But, because the enhancement

223 *See* Roberts, *supra* 157 at 416–17.

224 *See, e.g.*, Model Text for the Indian Bilateral Investment Treaty 2016, Art. 15.2, available at http://mof.gov.in/reports/ModelTextIndia_BIT.pdf (requiring investors seek relief before local judiciaries for at least five years prior to seeking international arbitration).

225 Roberts, *supra* note 157 at 416–17 (explaining that "South Africa recently terminated most of its investment treaties and replaced them with domestic legislation permitting foreign investors to litigate in its domestic courts or bring mediation claims against the government" and "Brazil has championed 'investment facilitation' agreements where an ombudsman is given powers to try to resolve disputes involving foreign investors. If the dispute persists, the treaty parties consent in advance to state-to-state arbitration").

of state control over ISA violates one of the central pacts of the Grand Bargain that produced ISA (the independence of the arbitral processes from judicial control), enhancing state control presents the most radical reform of ISA.[226]

Such a proposal would enhance judicial control to a level beyond the highly deferential review (if any substantive judicial review occurs at all, as none exists for arbitrations conducted under ICSID[227]) of arbitral awards that exists now. Enhanced control would not necessarily require direct de novo review, effectively resulting in the re-litigation of disputes in national courts. Enhanced control thus provides one means for legitimating the institution of ISA while retaining the institution's essential characteristics as an investor-initiated dispute *adjudicated* before an independent and impartial tribunal. Indeed, the calibration of the level of judicial review applied to non-judicial bodies performing judicial tasks has an extensive history as a means of legitimating actions of questionable democratic legitimacy outside the context of ISA. In the United States, for example, modulated levels of deferential review of administrative action serve to legitimate and enhance the quality of administration.[228]

And it is not farfetched to suggest that ISA is best understood as a system of global administrative governance; much like national public law, international investment law establishes a "legal framework for investor-state cooperation and in restricting governmental abuse of power, is functionally comparable to constitutional guarantees and administrative law principles at the domestic level that ensure nondiscrimination, government according to the rule of law, and respect for property rights."[229] Accordingly, modulated levels of judicial review (or deference to the arbitral tribunal's initial decision) could exist in a similar way to the deferential review of administrative decisions that courts employ in review of their own government's actions.

Such sliding scales of deference are not the only mode of enhancing judicial control over private arbitration. Indeed, a distinction can be made between ex ante and ex poste judicial controls of investor-state arbitration. The majority of existing mechanisms of control occur ex poste the provision of an arbitral

226 *See id.* (noting that some "states, most notably Brazil and South Africa, reject the legitimacy and utility of direct international claims by foreign investors against states ...").

227 "Where ICSID has jurisdiction, its decisions are final and are subject to review only within ICSID itself." *Micula v. Gov't of Romania*, 104 F. Supp. 3d 42, 45 (D.D.C. 2015).

228 *See, generally*, Adrian Vermeule, Law's Abnegation: From Law's Empire to the Administrative State (2017).

229 Schill, *supra* note 107 at 86. *See also* Kingsbury & Schill, *supra* note 11 at 1 (stating ISA "is also a structure of global governance" that helps "define specific principles of global administrative law and set standards for States in their internal administrative processes").

award, and take the form of party-initiated actions before national judiciaries to confirm or enforce or annul an arbitral award. But it is equally possible that designers of the system of international arbitration could create and enhance ex ante judicial controls over arbitration. To a certain extent, such controls already exist in anti-arbitration injunctions,[230] which prohibit a party from submitting a dispute to arbitration and require the judicial adjudication of the claim, and anti-suit injunctions, which require a party to submit a claim to arbitration and prohibit the judicial adjudication of a claim.[231]

Nor is the enhancement of judicial review necessarily antithetical to the institution of ISA. Judicial bodies already serve as one means of control over the system of investor-state arbitration;[232] when losing parties seek to annul (or victorious parties seek to enforce against uncooperative states) non-ICSID awards, the judiciaries of the state in which the parties placed the Seat of the Arbitration may review the arbitral award for error under the parameters provided by the New York Convention. Simultaneously, the judiciaries of the states in which an uncooperative losing party has assets may similarly review a non-ICSID arbitral award under a highly deferential standard to determine whether to enforce that award against the uncooperative losing party's assets.[233] In

---

230 *See, e.g.*, Ting-Wei Chiang, *Anti-Arbitration Injunctions in Investment Arbitration: Lessons Learnt from the* India v. Vodafone *Case*, 11 Contemp. Asia Arb. J. 251 (2018); John Joy, *Anti-Arbitration Injunctions: A Comparison of Approaches and the Problem of National Court Interference*, 3 Euro. Int'l Arb. Rev.

231 *See, generally*, S.I. Strong, *Anti-Suit Injunctions in Judicial and Arbitral Procedures in the United States*, 66 Am. J. Comp. L. (2018); Steven R. Swanson, *Antisuit Injunctions in Support of International Arbitration*, 81 TUL. L. REV. 395 (2006); Daniel Tan, *Anti-Suit Injunctions and the Vexing Problem of Comity*, 45 VA. J. INT'L L. 283 (2005); Emmanuel Gaillard, Reflections on the Use of Anti-Suit Injunctions in International Arbitration, in PERVASIVE PROBLEMS IN INTERNATIONAL ARBITRATION 203, 204–05 (Loukas Mistelis & Julian Lew eds., 2006).

232 W. Michael Reisman, Systems of Control in International Adjudication (1989) at 4–5 (explaining generally the role of judicial control over international adjudication).

233 The enforcement (or, less commonly, annulment) of ISA awards issued under UNCITRAL rules occurs pursuant to the New York Convention, which governs the enforcement of commercial arbitral awards. The New York Convention was implemented in the United States by amendment of the FAA. *See* Act of July 31, 1970, Pub.L. 91–368, 84 Stat. 692, codified at 9 U.S.C. §§ 201–208. The New York Convention governs the treatment of arbitral awards in the U.S., among 145 other states, and, "for all intents and purposes, that part of the world which is mostly actively engaged in international commercial arbitration" W. Michael Reisman & Brian Richardson, *Tribunals and Courts: An Interpretation of the Architecture of International Commercial Arbitration*, in Arbitration: Next Fifty Years, 21 (Albert Van Den Berg, ed., 2011). But, "[w]here ICSID has jurisdiction, its decisions are final and are subject to review only within ICSID itself." *Micula v. Gov't of Romania*, 104 F. Supp. 3d 42, 45 (D.D.C. 2015).

other words, ISAs conducted outside of ICSID do not occur in a judicial vacuum: awards are subject to actions enforcement and nullification by the states in which the parties agree to seat the arbitration, and any state in which the award need be enforced to become effective.

The ultimately insurmountable challenge for designers of a system of control vested with national judiciaries, however, is the obvious need to retain the benefits of investor-state arbitration, specifically the provision of a neutral mechanism for the resolution of investment disputes that would otherwise be geopolitically fraught, while still enhancing the democratic legitimacy of the institution. In other words, enhancing judicial review of ISA must not replace the adjudication before an independent tribunal that constitutes the essence of ISA with adjudication before the presumably partial national judiciaries that investors seek to avoid.

Enhancing judicial control of ISA as a solution to ISA's legitimacy crisis fails for this reason. Indeed, investor-initiated claims may involve challenges to an action taken or decision issued by the very national judiciary that would then be reviewing an award adjudicating that challenge. In *Loewen v. United States*, for example, the jury verdict rendered by a state court in the United States was challenged as a violation of the federal government's obligation to provide "fair and equitable treatment" to foreign investors.[234] While the legislation implementing the New York Convention ensures that a federal rather than state court in the United States would review an arbitral award adjudicating a dispute between an investor and the state court decision,[235] it is entirely possible that a federal court would instead by reviewing an investor's challenge to a federal court decision. Accordingly, enhancing judicial control exerted by the national judiciary of the respondent state undermines the promise of impartiality so central to the appeal of ISA for investors and capital-exporting states, undermining the finality promised by independent ISA.[236]

Merely seating the arbitration outside the respondent state would ensure that an impartial judiciary presides over the dispute. But parties may be reluctant to do so given costs and convenience. Far more importantly with regard to the democratic legitimacy challenge, however, is the fact that submitting

234 Loewen, ICSID Case No. ARB (AF)/98/3, Interim Award on Jurisdiction (Jan. 5, 2001), para. 2, http://www.naftaclaims.com.

235 *See* 9 U.S.C. § 203 (granting federal courts subject matter jurisdiction over actions to enforce and annul arbitral awards issued pursuant to the New York Convention).

236 Brower II, *supra* note 45 at 77 (arguing that "judicial review [] undermines the legitimacy of investor-state arbitration by impairing the capacity of the process to produce final (that is to say, 'determinate') outcomes.").

sovereign regulatory decisions to the judicial review of *another state's* judiciary would exacerbate rather than remedy the democratic legitimacy challenge to ISA. For obvious reasons, the judiciary of another state is entirely removed from the democratic processes of the state hosting the investment, and a determination from another state's judiciary on whether a host state violated its obligations to protect foreign investment would be no more democratically legitimate than the decision of a private arbitral tribunal. In fact, as state's at least have the ability to name one arbitrator on a three-arbitrator panel, review conducted by a foreign court would allow for meaningfully less democratic input than does the current system.

Accordingly, enhancing national judiciaries' control over ISA fails to retain the fundamental promise of ISA. Even if such reform could successfully enhance the democratic legitimacy of ISA, it would amount to nothing less than the destruction of ISA.

Conclusion: The Future of Investor State Arbitration

If ISA cannot guarantee its survival by either incremental, systemic, or paradigmatic reform, what can best ensure the institution's durability? In an attempt to answer that question, this conclusion will address the national political changes necessary to preserve the institution of investor-state arbitration. Because ISA cannot attain democratic legitimacy in the face of populist political challenges on theoretical grounds, as we suggest it cannot, the institution's survival depends upon the more equitable distribution of benefits that ISA promises to deliver: economic development and a more peaceful international order. In short, because ISA cannot guarantee its own survival through internal reform, efforts to establish the conditions for its durability depend upon *national* rather than *inter*national political action. We emphasize that this is a national rather than international political task because of the inadequacy of purely internationally-focused reform proposals intended to preserve the institution of ISA, whether by modifying the substance of investment protections or the process by which those investment protections are enforced. Although international law can help facilitate and encourage the more equitable distribution of resources in a general way, the precise contours of a state's internal distribution of resources across its population is a quintessentially *national* political task. This national political task can be understood as a response to the two distinct political challenges to ISA, though the each challenge cannot be addressed independently.

First, the economic political task necessary to preserve ISA requires the political legitimization of foreign investment, and global trade writ large, in response to the nationalist right's calls for protectionism across the traditionally capital-exporting world.[237] The political legitimization of foreign investment and foreign trade will rely upon the more equitable distribution of the undeniable gains wrought by such investment and trade across society. That globalization has exacerbated economic inequality is axiomatic;[238] but so too is the fact that such a distribution of the gains wrought by globalization is not inevitable, but rather the result of specific political decisions made on a national level. Because ISA retains as its primary goal increasing the availability and decreasing the cost of foreign capital, political support for the exportation (and importation) of foreign capital is a necessary condition for ISA to continue to develop. That political support depends upon the more equitable distribution of the benefits wrought by the free flow of capital.

Second is the political task of democratically legitimating ISA, which involves states obtaining the democratic approval of delegation of judicial power of state regulatory decisions to either private or supranational actors. As explained *supra* Part 3, such delegations are extremely difficult to theoretically justify, and mere modifications to the system of ISA either fail to resolve this problem, or preclude ISA from delivering on its fundamental promise of independent adjudication. Accordingly, any such legitimization must turn upon the institution's instrumental capacity to deliver the benefits it promises, and then the equitable distribution of those benefits across society at the national level. Again, this is a national rather than international legal task, and an extremely difficult one with regard to those benefits of ISA that are more difficult to quantify. To the extent ISA enhances economic development by increasing the availability of foreign investments for capital-intensive projects,[239] the wealth wrought by such projects can be better distributed across society through

237 Brower & Blanchard, *supra* note 53 at 763 (detailing how, "[a]fter decades of nearly universally increasing openness toward foreign investment, the last several years have brought an uptick in investment protectionism and a return to the discourse from the 1960s and 1970s about a 'New International Economic Order' and 'permanent sovereignty over natural re-sources.'").

238 *See, generally*, Francois Bourguignon, *Inequality and Globalization: How the Rich Get Richer as the Poor Catch Up*, Foreign Affairs (2016).

239 Puig, *supra* note 22 ("Under this theory, private FDI leads to economic growth and economic development. In order to encourage FDI, well-defined property rights adopted in different instruments of protection (i.e., relationship-specific contracts, foreign investment laws or investment treaties) shall be complemented by access to a functional dispute-settlement forum.").

taxation and other redistributive political programs. This is equally true of other benefits of increased flows of foreign investment, including "the transfer of technology connected to foreign investment, the creation of employment, [and] additional tax revenue."[240] And the fact that states continue to enter into investment agreements containing ISA provisions, including those agreements between states with existing but weaker investment protections demonstrates the success of the mechanism in promoting foreign investment.[241] Though profoundly difficult politically, the more equitable distribution of such economic benefits intra-nationally remains at least theoretically possible.

To the extent that ISA depoliticizes economic disputes, thereby creating a more peaceful international arena, however, it is extremely difficult to even ascertain, much less redistribute, such abstract benefits. This is equally true of other abstract benefits of ISA, such as the creation of "legal infrastructure of the functioning of a global market economy by protecting property rights, offering contract protection, [and] establishing nondiscrimination as a prerequisite for competition through national and most-favored-nation treatment."[242] Enhancing democratic support for an institution with such diffuse benefits requires a concerted political effort, but the continued existence of ISA requires it.

References

Adkins, Cory & David S. Grewal, *Democracy and Legitimacy in Investor-State Arbitration*, 126 Yale L. J. FORUM (2016).

Afilalo, Ari, *Towards a Common Law of International Investment: How NAFTA Chapter 11 Panels Should Solve Their Legitimacy Crisis*, 17 Georgetown Int'l Envt'l L. Rev. (2004) p. 51.

Afilalo, Ari, *Meaning, Ambiguity and Legitimacy: Judicial (Re-)construction of NAFTA Chapter 11*, 25 Nw. J. Int'l L. & Bus. (2005) p. 279 at p. 282.

Arato, Julian, Corporations as Lawmakers, 56 HARV. INT'L L. J. 229, 231 (2015).

240 Brower & Schill, *supra* note 89 at 494–95.

241 Charles N. Brower, Sadie Blanchard, *What's in a Meme? The Truth about Investor-State Arbitration: Why It Need Not, and Must Not, Be Repossessed by States*, 52 Colum. J. Transnat'l L. 689, 701–702 (2014) (explaining that states' continued willingness to enter into investment agreements that in many cases strengthen the rights afforded to investors in comparison to past agreements demonstrates the success of the investor-state dispute resolution mechanism in promoting foreign investment).

242 *Id.*

Article 14.2(4), Agreement between the United States of America, the United Mexican States, and Canada 7/1/20.

Alabama Claims Case, Decision and Award (Sept. 14, 1872), reprinted in Thomas Willing Balch, The Alabama Arbitration, 131 app. (1900).

Alvarez, Guillermo Aguilar & Park, William W., *The New Face of Investment Arbitration: NAFTA Chapter 11*, 28 Yale J. Int'l L. 365, 366 (2003).

Alvarez, José & Gustavo Topalian, *The Paradoxical Argentina Cases*, 6 World Arb. & Mediation Rev. 491, 494 (2012).

H.E. Shahid Bashir, "WTO Dispute Settlement Body Developments in 2012," available at: https://www.wto.org/english/tratop_e/dispu_e/bashir_13_e.htm.

Behn, D., *Legitimacy, Evolution, and Growth in Investment Treaty Arbitration: Empirically Evaluating the State-of-the-Art*, 46(2) Georgetown Journal of International Law (2015).

Bellak, Christian, *How Bilateral Investment Treaties Impact on Foreign Direct Investment: A Meta-Analysis of Public Policy* (2013), *available* at http://www2.gre.ac.uk/__data/assets/pdf_file/0006/822705/Christian-Bellak-How-BilateralInvestment-Treaties-Impact-on-Foreign-Direct-Investment-A-Meta-analysis-of-Public-Policy.pdf.

Bhagwati, Jagdish, *The Capital Myth: The Difference Between Trade in Widgets and Dollars*, FOREIGN AFF., May-June 1998.

Bradner, Eric, Trump's TPP Withdrawal: 5 Things to Know, CNN, available at: https://www.cnn.com/2017/01/23/politics/trump-tpp-things-to-know/index.html.

Bourguignon, Francois, Inequality and Globalization: How the Rich Get Richer as the Poor Catch Up, Foreign Affairs (2016).

Brower, Charles H. II, *Structure, Legitimacy, and NAFTA's Investment Chapter*, 36 Vand. J. of Transnat'l L. 37, 89 (2003).

Brower, Charles N., Sadie Blanchard, What's in a Meme? The Truth about Investor-State Arbitration: Why It Need Not, and Must Not, Be Repossessed by States, 52 Colum. J. Transnat'l L. 689, 757 (2014).

Brower, Charles N., *A Crisis of Legitimacy*, Nat'l L. J. (7 Oct 2002).

Brower, Charles N., Charles H. Brower II and Jeremy K. Sharpe, *The Coming Crisis in the Global Adjudication System*, 19 Arb. Int'l (2003) p. 415.

Brower, Charles N., Jawad Ahmad, *Why the 'Demolition Derby' That Seeks to Destroy Investor-State Arbitration?*, 91 S. Cal. L. Rev. 1139, 1182 (2018).

Brower, Charles N., Stephan W. Schill, *Is Arbitration a Threat or a Boon to the Legitimacy of International Investment Law?*, 9 Chi. J. Int'l L. 471, 474–75 (2009).

Bucheler, Gebhard, Proportionality in Investor-State Arbitration, Oxford University Press: 2015, at Ch. 2, Investor-State Arbitration and the Argentine Cases.

CANACAR v. United States of America, https://investmentpolicyhub.unctad.org/ISDS/Details/348.

Caporal, Jack & William Alan Reinsch, "From NAFTA to USMCA: What's New and What's Next?," (October 3, 2018), available at: https://www.csis.org/analysis/nafta-usmca-whats-new-and-whats-next.

Clark, Grover, *The English Practice with Regard to Reprisals by Private Persons*, 27 AM. J. INT'L L. 694, 695–96 (1933).

Cheng, Tai-Heng, *Precedent and Control in Investment Treaty Arbitration*, 30 Ford. J. Int'l L. 1014, 1016 (2009).

Chiang, Ting-Wei, *Anti-Arbitration Injunctions in Investment Arbitration: Lessons Learnt from the* India v. Vodafone *Case*, 11 Contemp. Asia Arb. J. 251 (2018).

Chung, Olivia, *The Lopsided International Investment Law Regime and Its Effect on the Future of Investor-State Arbitration*, 47 Va. J. Int'l L. (2007) p. 953.

Clayton v. Government of Canada, Award on Jurisdiction and Liability, Case No. 2009–04, ¶¶ 601–602 (Perm. Ct. Arb. 2015), http://www.pcacases.com/web/sendAttach/1287.

Corn Products Int'l, Inc. v. Mexico, ICSID Case No. ARB(AF)/04/01, Decision on Responsibility, Sep. Op. Arbitrator Lowenfeld, para. 1 (Jan. 15, 2008).

Coyle, John F., The Treaty of Friendship, Commerce and Navigation in the Modern Era, 51 Colum. J. Transnat'l L. 302, 327 (2013).

Dolzer, Rudolf & Christoph Schreuer, PRINCIPLES OF INTERNATIONAL INVESTMENT LAW 224 (2008).

Donnan, Shawn, NAFTA: Bitter Differences over Nafta Break into the Open, FINANCIAL TIMES (Oct. 18, 2017), https://www.ft.com/content/058aa538-b387-11e7-a398-73d59db9e399.

Eisenberg, Theodore, *Testing the Selection Effect: A New Theoretical Framework with Empirical Tests*, 19 J. Legal Stud. 339 (1990).

European Commission, Investment in TTIP and Beyond—The Path for Reform, Enhancing the Right to Regulate and Moving from Current ad hoc Arbitration Towards an Investment Court, at 11 (May 2015), available at http://trade.ec.europa.eu/doclib/docs/2015/may/tradoc_153408.PDF.

EUROPEAN PARLIAMENTARY RESEARCH SERVICE BRIEFING, INVESTOR-STATE DISPUTE SETTLEMENT: STATE OF PLAY AND PROSPECTS FOR REFORM (2014).

Franck, Susan D., *The Legitimacy Crisis in Investment Treaty Arbitration: Privatizing Public International Law Through Inconsistent Decisions*, 73 Fordham L. Rev. 1521, 1625 n.16 (2005).

Franck, Susan D., The ICSID Effect? Considering Potential Variations in Arbitration Awards, 51 VA. J. INT'L L. 825, 852 (2011).

Franck, Susan D., Lindsey E. Wylie, *Predicting Outcomes in Investment Treaty Arbitration*, 65 Duke L.J. 459, 461 (2015).

Franck, Susan D., *Development and Outcomes of Investment Treaty Arbitration*, 50 Harv. J. Int'l L. 435, 440 (2009).

Freeman, Samuel, *Constitutional Democracy and Legitimacy of Judicial Review*, 9 L. and Phil. 327 (1990).

Gaillard, Emmanuel, Reflections on the Use of Anti-Suit Injunctions in International Arbitration, in PERVASIVE PROBLEMS IN INTERNATIONAL ARBITRATION 203, 204–05 (Loukas Mistelis & Julian Lew eds., 2006).

Glaberson, William, NAFTA Invoked to Challenge Court Award, N.Y. TIMES, Jan. 28, 1999, at C6, available at http://www.nytimes.com/1999/01/28/business/nafta-invoked-to-challenge-court-award.html? pagewanted=print.

Goldhaber, Michael D., Big Arbitrations, Focus Eur., Summer 2003, at 22 available at http://www.americanlawyer.com/focuseurope/bigarbitrations.html.

Goldhaber, Michael D., *The Rise of Arbitral Power Over Domestic Courts*, 1 Stan. J. of Complex Lit. 373, 416 (2013).

Goetz, Antoine & Consorts et S.A. Affinage des Metaux v. Republique du Burundi, ICSID Case No. ARB/01/2, Sentence, ¶¶ 278–79 (June 21, 2012), *available at* http://www.italaw.com/sites/default/files/case-documents/italaw1086.pdf; Inmaris Perestroika Sailing Maritime Services GmbH v. Ukraine, ICSID Case No. ARB/08/8, Award, 431–32 (Mar. 1, 2012), *available at* https://icsid.worldbank.org/ICSID/FrontServlet?requestType=CasesRH&actionVal=showDoc&docId=DC3296_En&caseId=C320.

Greenwood, Christopher, http://arbitrationblog.kluwerarbitration.com/2018/11/30/does-investor-state-arbitration-have-a-future-keynote-speech-by-sir-christopher-greenwood/.

Gurudevan, *Naveen, An Evaluation of Current Legitimacy-based Objections to NAFTA's Chapter 11 Investment Dispute Resolution Process*, 6 San Diego Int'l L. J. (2005) p. 399.

Hague Convention on the Limitation of Employment of Force for Recovery of Contract Debts (opened for signature 18 October 1907, entered into force 26 January 1910).

Harten, Gus van, Investment Treaty Arbitration and Public Law (Oxford 2007).

Harten, Gus van, *Arbitrator Behaviour in Asymmetrical Adjudication: An Empirical Study of Investment Treaty Arbitration*, 50 Osgoode Hall Law Journal 211 (2012).

Hueckel, Rebalancing Legitimacy and Sovereignty in International Investment Agreements, 61 EMORY LJ. 601, 606 (2012).

International Bar Association Report, Consistency Efficiency and Transparency in Investment Treaty Arbitration (Nov. 2018).

Janssen, Andre & Wahnschaffe, Christian Johannes, *For Whom the Bell Tolls: Any Hope Left for Investment Arbitration After* Achmea?, Dispute Resolution in China, Europe and World (ed. Lei Chen and Andre Janssen) (Springer 2020).

Jones, Ray C., *NAFTA Chapter 11 Investor-to-State Dispute Resolution: A Shield to Be Embraced or a Sword to Be Feared?*, 2002 BYU L. Rev. 527, 529–31.

Joy, John, *Anti-Arbitration Injunctions: A Comparison of Approaches and the Problem of National Court Interference*, 3 Euro. Int'l Arb. Rev.

Joint Interpretative Instrument on the Comprehensive Economic and Trade Agreement (CETA) Between Canada and the European Union and its Member States, OJ L 11, 14 (Jan. 2017).

Kaufman, Dan, "Did Scott Walker and Donald Trump Deal Away the Wisconsin Governor's Race to Foxconn?", The New Yorker, Nov. 3, 2018.

Kaufmann-Kohler, Gabrielle, 'Is Consistency a Myth?' in Emmanuel Gaillard and Yas Banifatemi (eds), Int'l Arbitration Inst, Precedent in International Arbitration (Juris Publishing, Inc 2008).

Kaufmann-Kohler, Gabrielle, Interpretive Powers of the Free Trade Commission and the Rule of Law, in Fifteen Years of NAFTA Chapter 11 Arbitration (2011).

Kingsbury, Benedict, & Schill, Stephan, *Investor-State Arbitration as Governance: Fair and Equitable Treatment, Proportionality and the Emerging Global Administrative Law*, *TDM 2* (*2011*).

Laird, Ian & Rebecca Askew, *Finality Versus Consistency: Does Investor-State Arbitration Need an Appellate System*; 7 J. App. Practice Proc. 285 (2005).

Langford, Malcolm & Daniel Behn, *Managing Backlash: The Evolving Investment Treaty Arbitrator?*, European Journal of Int'l L. 6 (2016).

Langford, Malcolm, Daniel Behn, Runar Hilleren Lie, *The Revolving Door in International Investment Arbitration*, 20 Journal of Int'l Econ. Law 301 (2017).

Micula v. Gov't of Romania, 104 F. Supp. 3d 42, 45 (D.D.C. 2015).

Leal-Arcas, Rafael, *Proliferation of Regional Trade Agreements: Complementing or Supplanting Multilateralism*, 11 Chi. J. Int'l L. 597 (2011).

Legum, Barton, Federalism, *NAFTA Chapter Eleven and the Jay Treaty of 1794*, 95 AM. SOC. INT'L. L. PROC. 202 (2001).

Loewen, ICSID Case No. ARB (AF)/98/3, Interim Award on Jurisdiction (Jan. 5, 2001), para. 2, http:// www.naftaclaims.com.

Lowe, Vaughan, Private Disputes and the Public Interest in International Law, in INTERNATIONAL LAW AND DISPUTE SETTLEMENT: NEW PROBLEMS AND TECHNIQUES 3, 10 (Duncan French et al. eds., 2010).

Matiation, Stefan, *Arbitration With Two Twists: Loewen v. United States and Free Trade Commission Intervention in NAFTA Chapter 11 Disputes*, 24 U. Pa. J. Int'l Econ. L. 452, 453 (2003).

Meyer, Timothy and Ganesh Sitaraman, A Blueprint for a New American Trade Policy, Dec. 2018.

Miles, Kate, The Origins of International Investment Law: Empire, Environment and the Safeguarding of Capital (2013).

NAFTA, art. 1105(1).

Opinion 1/17 of the Court of Justice of the European Union, (Apr. 30, 2019), *available at*: http://curia.europa.eu/juris/document/document.jsf?text=&docid=213502&pageIndex=0&doclang=EN&mode=lst&dir=&occ=first&part=1&cid=4976548.

Orecki, Marcin. 2017. Bye-Bye BITs? Poland Reviews Its Investment Policy. *Kluwer Arbitration Blog.* Available at <http://kluwerarbitrationblog.com/2017/01/31/bye-bye-bits-poland-reviews-investment-policy/>.

Parra, Antonio R., THE HISTORY OF ICSID 66–67 (2012).

Paulsson, Jan, International Arbitration and the Generation of Legal Norms, Transnat'l Di. Mgmt., Dec. 2006, at 5 n.3.

Peterson, Luke Eric, Bilateral Investment Treaties and Development Policy-Making 1–2, available at http://www.iisd.org/pdf/2004/trade-bits.pdf.

Phillip Morris Asia Ltd. v. Australia, Case No. 2012–12, Award on Jurisdiction and Admissibility (Perm. Ct. Arb. 2015).

Piketty, Thomas, LE CAPITAL AU XXI SIECLE 120–21 (2013).

Pomeroy, Adam R., *Penn Central After 35 Years: A Three Part Balancing Test or a One Strike Rule*, 22 FED CIR. B.J. 677, 698 (2012).

Posner, Eric A., *Liberal Internationalism and the Populist Backlash*, 49 Ariz. St. L. J. 795, 813 (2018).

Press Release, United Nations Information Service, UNCITRAL Adopts Transparency Rules for Treaty-Based Investor-State Arbitration and Amends the UNCITRAL Arbitration Rules (Dec. 18, 2013), available at http://www.unis.unvienna.org/unis/pressrels/2013/unisl186.html.

Priest, George L. & Benjamin Klein, *The Selection of Disputes for Litigation*, 13 J. Legal Stud. 1 (1984).

Puig, Sergio, *Recasting ICSID's Legitimacy Debate—Towards a Goal-Based Empirical Agenda*, 36 Ford. Int'l L. J. 465, 479–480 (2013).

Puig, Sergio and Gregory Shaffer, *Imperfect Alternatives: Institutional Choice and the Reform of Investment Law*, 112 Am. J. Int'l L. 361, 364 (2018).

Reisman, W. Michael, *The Past and Future of the Great Compact*, 33 ICSID Rev. 1, 56 (2018).

Reisman, W. Michael, *International Investment Arbitration and ADR: Married but Best Living Apart*, 24 ICSID Rev. 185 (2009).

Reisman, W. Michael, Systems of Control in International Adjudication (1989) at 4–5.

Reisman, W. Michael & Brian Richardson, *Tribunals and Courts: An Interpretation of the Architecture of International Commercial Arbitration*, in Arbitration: Next Fifty Years, 21 (Albert Van Den Berg, ed., 2011).

Resar, Alexander W., *The Evolution of Investor-State Arbitration in the Trans-Pacific Partnership Agreement*, 34 Berkeley J. Int'l L. 159, 162–63 (2016).

Reynoso, Isabella, "Spain's Renewable Energy Saga: Lessons for international investment law and sustainable development," Investment Treaty News: International Institute for Sustainable Development (June 27, 2019), *available at*: https://www.iisd.org/itn/en/2019/06/27/spains-renewable-energy-saga-lessons-for-international-investment-law-and-sustainable-development-isabella-reynoso/.

Roberts, Anthea, *Triangular Treaties: The Extent and Limits of Investment Treaty Rights*, 56 Harv. Int'l L.J. 353, 360 (2015).

Roberts, Anthea, *Incremental Systemic and Paradigmatic Reform of Investor-State Arbitration*, 112 Am. J. Int'l L. 410, 416–17 (2018).

Rogers, Catherine, *Emerging Dilemmas in International Economic Arbitration: The Vocation of the International Arbitrator*, 20 AM. U. INT'L L. Rev. 957, 965 (2005).

Roosevelt, Theodore, 'Sixth Annual Message to the Senate and House of Representatives' (3 December 1906) http://www.presidency.ucsb.edu/ws/?pid=29547.

Roussalis v. Romania, ICSID ARB/06/01, Award, 868, 872 (Dec. 7, 2011), available at http://www.italaw.com/sites/default/files/case-documents/ita0723.pdf.

Rubenfeld, Jed, *Unilateralism and Constitutionalism*, 78 N.Y.U. L. Rev. 1971, 2007 (2004).

Sadurski, Wojciech, *Democratic Legitimacy of the European Union: A Diagnosis and Some Modest Proposals*, 32 Pol. Ybk of Int'l L. (2013).

Schill, Stephan, *Multilateralizing Investment Treaties through Most-Favored-Nation Clauses*, 27 Berkely J. Int'l L. 496, 561 (2009).

Schill, Stephan W., *International Investment Law's Legitimacy*, 52 Va. J. Int'l L. 57, 67 (2011).

Schneiderman, David, *NAFTA's Takings Rule: American Constitutionalism Comes to Canada*, 46 U. TORONTO L.J. 499, 503 (1996).

Schultz, Thomas and Cedric Dupont, *Investment Arbitration: Promoting the Rule of Law or Over-Empowering Investors? A Quantitative Empirical Study*, 25 European Journal of International Law 1147 (2014).

Schwebel, Stephen M., Keynote Address: In Defence of Bilateral Investment Treaties, at 2, available at http://www.arbitration-icca.org/media/2/14169776244680/schwebel_in_defence_of_bits.pdf.

Sornarajah, M., "A Coming Crisis: Expansionary Trends in Investment Treaty Arbitration" in Karl P. Sauvant, ed., Appeals Mechanism in International Investment Disputes (2008) pp. 39–45.

Sornarajah, M., *The Descent into Normlessness*, in EVOLUTION IN INVESTMENT TREATY LAW AND ARBITRATION 631, 640 (Chester Brown & Kate Miles eds., 2012).

Spears, Suzanne A., The Quest for Policy Space in a New Generation of International Investment Agreements, 13 J. INT'L ECON. L. 1037, 1071 (2010).

Strong, S.I., *Anti-Suit Injunctions in Judicial and Arbitral Procedures in the United States*, 66 Am. J. Comp. L. (2018).

Sweet, Alec Stone & Florian Grisel, The Evolution of International Arbitration: Judicialization, Governance, Legitimacy 190 (2017).

Sweet, Alec Stone, Michael Yunsuck Chung & Adam Saltzman, *Arbitral Lawmaking and State Power: An Empirical Analysis of Investment Arbitration*, 7 J. INT'L DISP. SETTLEMENT 1, 16–17 (2017).

Summers, Lionel M., *Arbitration and Latin America*, 3 Cal. W. L.J. 1, 6–7 (2001).

Swanson, Steven R., Antisuit *Injunctions in Support of International Arbitration*, 81 TUL. L. REV. 395 (2006).

Tan, Daniel, *Anti-Suit Injunctions and the Vexing Problem of Comity*, 45 VA. J. INT'L L. 283 (2005).

Tecnicas Medioambientales Teemed SA v The United Mexican States, ICSID Case No ARB(AF)/00/2, Award of (May 29, 2003) 119, available online at <http://icsid.world bank.org/ICSID/.

Tienhaara, Kyla, Regulatory Chill and the Threat of Arbitration: A View from Political Science, in EVOLUTION IN INVESTMENT TREATY LAW AND ARBITRATION 606, 606 (Chester Brown & Kate Miles eds., 2011).

TransCanada Keystone Pipeline, LP v. John Kerry, Complaint, Case 4:16-cv-00036 (S.D. Tex. filed Jan. 6, 2016).

Treaty of Amity, Commerce and Navigation, Nov. 19, 1794, U.S.-Gr. Brit., 8 Stat. 116.

Tung, Ko-Yung, *Investor-State Dispute Settlement under the Trans-Pacific Partnership*, 23 Cal. Int'l L. J. 19, 22 (2015).

UNCITRAL Rules on Transparency in Treaty-based Investor-State Arbitration, UNCTIRAL (Jan. 2014), available at http://www.uncitral.org/pdf/english/texts/arbitration/rules-on-transparency/pre-release-UNCITRAL-Rules-on-Transparency.pdf.

U.N. General Assembly Charter of Economic Right and Duties of States (CERDS), GA Resolution A/Res/40/182 (17 December 1984).

U.N. G.A. Res. 3281, U.N. GAOR, 29th Sess., Supp. No. 31, at 50, U.N. Doc. A/9631 (1974).

U.N. Conference on Trade and Development ("UNCTAD"), Bilateral Investment Treaties in the Mid-1990s, at 18–19, U.N. Doc. UNCTAD/ITE/IIT/7, U.N. Sales No. E.98.II.D.8 (1998).

UN General Assembly's Declaration on the Establishment of a New International Economic Order. GA Resolution A/RES/S-6/3201 (1 May 1974).

United States Trade Representative Robert Lighthizer's testimony at a House Ways and Means Hearing, available at: https://worldtradelaw.typepad.com/ielpblog/2018/03/brady-lighthizer-isds-exchange.html.

Vandevelde, Kenneth J., *A Brief History of International Investment Agreements*, 12 U.C. DAVIS J. INT'L L. & POL'Y 157, 168–70 (2005).

Vermeule, Adrian, LAW'S ABNEGATION: FROM LAW'S EMPIRE TO THE ADMINISTRATIVE STATE (2017).

Viñuales, Jorge, *Foreign Investment and the Environment in International Law* (Cambridge: Cambridge University Press, 2012).

Voeten, Erik, Populism and Backlashes against International Courts, Perspectives on Politics, Volume 18, Issue 2, June 2020, pp. 407–422.

Weber, Max, Economy and Society: An Outline of Interpretive Sociology (Guenther Roth and Claus Wittich eds., 1968).

Yackee, Jason Webb, The First Investor-State Arbitration: The Suez Canal Company v Egypt (1864), 17 J. WORLD INV. & TRADE 401 (2016).

Yackee, Jason Webb, *Pacta Sant Servanda and State Promises to Foreign Investors Before Bilateral Investment Treaties: Myth and Reality*, 32 FORDHAM INT'L LJ. 1550, 1610–11 (2008).

www.ingramcontent.com/pod-product-compliance
Lightning Source LLC
Chambersburg PA
CBHW031331230926
51848CB00001B/185
9789004390584